MW01480509

My "Plane" Truth

A Soul Satisfying Crash Course to
Unconditional Love and Forgiveness

Jill Douglas

authorHOUSE®

AuthorHouse™
1663 Liberty Drive
Bloomington, IN 47403
www.authorhouse.com
Phone: 1-800-839-8640

First published by AuthorHouse 2/14/2012

ISBN: 978-1-4678-7000-9 (e)
ISBN: 978-1-4678-7001-6 (hc)
ISBN: 978-1-4678-7002-3 (sc)

Library of Congress Control Number: 2011960219

Printed in the United States of America

Any people depicted in stock imagery provided by Thinkstock are models, and such images are being used for illustrative purposes only. Certain stock imagery © Thinkstock.

This book is printed on acid-free paper.

Front Cover Picture taken Jan. 22, 2006 - Copyright Shane Power

Table of Contents

Dedication   vii

Acknowledgments   ix

Introduction
My Life: Coincidence or Fate?   xiii

Part One: The Early Years
Chapter One—A Change of Destiny   3

Chapter Two—My Hole-in-One Duck Dream   8

Chapter Three—The Performance Begins   13

Chapter Four—The Ghosts of Christmas Past   26

Chapter Five—Weighing In on Image: My Teenage Years   31

Chapter Six—To Burn or Not to Burn My Bra:
Is That Really the Question?   36

Chapter Seven—Power & Work Addiction: Owning It   47

Chapter Eight—The Worse Got the Better of Me   51

Part Two: My Princess Life With Terry
Chapter Nine—Finding Jilly, Like a Leaf Blowing in the Wind   61

Chapter Ten—Straight Up the Mountain of Happiness ...
One Step at a Time   69

Chapter Eleven—Trekking in India:
My Soul's Journey Continues   74

Chapter Twelve—Nudges from God:
The Owl in the Burnt Out Tree   86

Chapter Thirteen—The Lure of Storm Watching   90

Part Three: Rescue and Recovery

Chapter Fourteen—The Miraculous Rescue 117

Chapter Fifteen—The Transition Home to Edmonton 125

Chapter Sixteen—My Team of Angels 131

Chapter Seventeen—Simplify: Every Day is a Diamond Day 138

Chapter Eighteen—Back Home to My New Reality 147

Part Four: My Spiritual Transformation Begins

Chapter Nineteen—Limiting Beliefs 153

Chapter Twenty—Feathers, Coins, and Other
Messages From Above 158

Chapter Twenty-One—Inside The Vortex 162

Chapter Twenty-Two—Learning To Meditate: An Inside Job 165

Chapter Twenty-Three—An Empty Canvas for My Emotional
Healing to Begin 172

Chapter Twenty-Four—As If God's Hands Were On Mine 179

Chapter Twenty-Five—Brave Heart: My Love Story 181

Chapter Twenty-Six—Synchronistic Events 186

Chapter Twenty-Seven—Exposing The Truth 189

Chapter Twenty-Eight—Steady Pose, Full Breath, and
Awareness 192

Chapter Twenty-Nine—The Crack in the Sidewalk: A Full-
Circle Forgiving Moment 198

Epilogue 205

Resources 209

Dedication

Terry 24 hours before his death – Wickaninnish Inn

This book is dedicated to Terry Douglas. "Thank you" doesn't seem to convey all the heartfelt appreciation and joyousness I want to express to you for sharing your love and life with me. You have made the continuation of my journey so much easier, and for that I am eternally grateful. May you rest in peace … until we meet, laugh, and love again?

Respectfully to Edward Huggett, the pilot, who passed, and to the young boy, whose family wishes to remain anonymous: I know your loved ones sadly miss you … but you will not be forgotten.

Finally to the other survivors—Stacey Curtiss, Melissa Richmond who I keep in touch with and to the Mom and young girl who wish to remain anonymous—I hope you find the courage to continue with your life in the fullest way possible.

Acknowledgments

I'd like first to acknowledge the Search and Rescue Squadron team (SARS), who carefully plucked all five survivors off the mountain under extremely dangerous conditions. I know you were all just doing your jobs that day, but you need to know that every life you save is a measure of heroics. Thank you to the team of dedicated nurses and doctors who responded so remarkably to our emergency that fateful day.

I also offer huge thanks to my team of angels back home in Edmonton. I feel a great sense of indebtedness to all who reached out to help me in my greatest hours of need. At the top of the long list is Laurie McClelland from St. Albert. Every day, I felt your unconditional love in supporting me. Your special touch in caring for me at the U of A hospital, and your diligence in just getting things looked after long after I was out of the hospitals—all because you had a friend in dire need—moved me greatly. I will be especially thankful for what you, Brian, and Morgan did for me. While we live apart now, I hope that you know my heart knows your heart. I am so thankful and grateful for the time we did have together, when we would giggle ourselves silly. Thank you also for allowing me to move on with my new life.

My second angel is Lois Vance, from Kingston. You single handedly guided me back to emotional stability by supporting my newfound spirituality. I loved your "special touch" foot massages. You were and are my biggest supporter, and I feel honored to consider you my sister. Love emanates from every pore of your body and spreads to all those lucky enough to be in your sphere. You helped me understand that all of this tragedy was for one thing only: to find, know and love the person I really am.

To John Pike, my third "business" angel, as they say, the show must go on, but you so lovingly took great care to make sure that not only were Terry's employees looked after, but also that my future was secure. Only a unique person like you, John, could handle the myriad details and complex set of circumstances to prepare Terry's store for changeover. I am eternally grateful for all your learned wisdom and guidance. You treated everyone with compassion, fairness and dignity. Thank you to Marjorie for supporting John while he supported my family and me.

Long after I was out of the hospitals, my wonderful friends never forgot about me. I know they did it all from their hearts, and I thank them all (in no particular order): Shirley and George Vallance, Linda and Owen DeBathe, Meagan Badger, Emily Fabre, Doug McClelland, Karen Kelley, Sylvia Chipchura, Liz Clarke, Janet Robinson, Maxine Alguire, Pat and Ron Prior, Jean and Keith Fraser, Jan and Dave Reidie, Elaine and Roland Reynaud, Pat and Jos Reynhoudt, Andrea and Keith Gostlin, Garian and Eric Sellors, Joanne and Del Blanchette, Ron and Wendy Berlando, Sylvia and Jim Mayne, the thirty or more 'Flower Power' people, Gary and Jane Banks, Stew Begg, Bonnie Boucher, Dr. Bill and Jennifer Mackie, Dr. Jim and Patti Metcalfe, Dr. Guy Lavoie, Dr. Robert Stiegelmar, Dr. Angela Scharfenberger, Carol and Dan Villeneuve, Ken and Patty Cleall, Myrna McLaughlin, Myrna Douziech, Dallas and Joy Mowat, Eileen and Fred Filthaut, Dan and Carol Pelletier, Bev and Terry Loat, Judy and Bob Carwell, Debbie and Stewart Bruce, Carol DeBathe and John Podger, Jeananne and Pat Kirwin, Donna and John Crozier, Linda and Dave Campbell, Jack Thurbon, to my entire bridge ladies group, Betty Hillier, Elinor Thubron, Terry Corbett, Deanna Nemirsky, Marci Sharpe, Brenda Sutherland, Louise Wong, Rick Kennedy, Ash Khan, Damian Gynane, Arley Elliott, Mackenzie and Laura Kyle, Dean and Nod Kyle, Jack and Jill Juusola, Ron Hlady, Margaret Tkachuk, John and Marjorie Pike, Ted Romanowski, Vernon Forster, Carole and Gerry Feist, Joanne Ness and Cuyler, Dr. Greg Kuruliak, Dr. Darcy Zalasky, Dr. Rob Mutch, Dr. Manji, Dr. Pawa, Dr. Sandby, Dave Oakie, Curt Chambers, Dr. Mike Schmidt, Kip Petch, Megan Murphy, Sharon Matthews, Jane Tielker, J.J. Camp, Joe Fiorante, Trent Hammans, Patti Shannon, John Sharp and Darlene Montgomery.

To Robin, my spiritual partner who so beautifully mirrors me if I veer even ever so slightly off the path to finding out and expressing who we really are: I would never have known, if I didn't see it in your eyes so clearly, how much I could love and be loved.

Beverly Lenz, Taylor Wideman, Daniella DiMarchie, Frankie Johns, Jesai Chantler, Christy Crain—my healers. Your gifts are unique and generously shared. I am so grateful for your insights and your willingness to support me on my healing journey.

To my family, my dad, Brian Badger; my mom, Gerry Badger; my brother Steve, his wife Jeanette, and my nieces Carrie and Melissa; and my other brother Rick Badger, and my niece Meagan. Thank you for all your efforts in helping me through the transition back to my new normal. While we may never agree on certain things or events in our lives, I respect and honor our individual paths, which will eventually lead us all back to our true selves ... our soul selves.

To (Aunt) Jerry and (Uncle) Gordon Stenhouse, (Uncle) Wayne and (Aunt) Trudy Badger; my cousins Malinda Van Aalst, Derek, and Geoff Badger and to Jim, Gregory, Russell, and Ashleigh Vance ... thank you for just being supportive in any way you could.

To my stepsons, Kevin and Craig Douglas, you should know that my sorrow is hard to express, as I am saddened that you had to lose your father so suddenly and that your lives were also changed instantly. If I can say one thing, it's that I know Terry was very proud of you both and always wanted nothing but happiness for each of you on your chosen life paths; as do I. Tragedy has separated us, but the memories will always be ours to cherish. I am grateful for the years we shared as a blended family.

Craig, Terry and Kevin Xmas 2005

In a few cases, some names have been changed at the request of the individuals.

Last, and certainly not least ... to God! Thanks for always loving me and showing me the way.

Introduction

My Life: Coincidence or Fate?

"There is one thing in this world that you must never forget to do. If you forget everything else and not this, there's nothing to worry about; but if you remember everything else and forget this, then you will have done nothing in your life."

Rumi

Many of the saints spent their lives searching for that grain of truth that would give them a sense of meaning, of a purpose beyond everyday toil and strife. For all of my twenties, most of my thirties, and some of my forties, I was very much on the fast track to nowhere, at least not to my soul's desire. Admittedly, after a few different career directions, I finally took steps towards realizing my childhood dream of being an interior designer. It took until my early forties before I honestly thought I had found my true purpose—or, at least, I had convinced myself that I was living my purpose and thus on the road to happiness.

Spiritually, I was nowhere close to being satisfied. From the outside things looked really good: I finally had all the stuff I had been working so hard to acquire. However, the inside job, the *real* me, was still floundering. In fact, I couldn't have been further from the truth of the real purpose of my life.

Like many people today, I searched high and low for the answers to age-old questions. *What is my purpose in life? How do I find it? How will I know if I find it? More importantly, how do I find true happiness?* It occurred to me only after the plane crash that perhaps the truth could not be found by the mind alone. Nor did it have anything to do with all the external pursuits of career and stuff; I had spent my life chasing.

My first foray into the spiritual world, as I knew it, occurred when I was twenty-one. I was somehow put in touch with a medium (although at that time, I would have described him as a psychic). This foray was certainly outside my comfort zone, so I kept his reading to myself for many years. Eventually, as my spiritual quest grew, I did share my experience with a few like-minded friends, long before the events described in the reading came true. Regardless, the experience never left me; yet, I do not feel it unduly influenced any of my life decisions.

This medium had the ability to see into and read the *akashic* records, which are a complete written account of each soul's agreements *before* they incarnate into this world. These records are reviewed again when a soul crosses over. I had never heard of the akashic records, let alone understood the concept that my whole life had already been written for me ... *by* me!

That spring day, I sat in wide-eyed, skeptical silence, as this male figure started to go into some sort of trance. Ten minutes passed before he started to talk to me. When he was ready, he indicated that I could now ask my questions.

My first question was, "Will I get married?"

"Yes," he answered—but the way he said it, I sensed there was more.

"Will I be married more than once?

"Yes," he matter-of-factly answered again.

Startled, I quickly changed the subject to my health. I was young, and hadn't even started to contemplate my first marriage, let alone a second. I didn't want to know if it could be even worse with regards to my love life. Divorce equated to failure to me at that time and I did not want to accept that I could potentially fail. I would have been more shocked to learn that two marriages would actually become three.

Upon my changing subjects, he again went silent, taking several more minutes before beginning to speak. He said, "You will have some serious health concerns around your mid- to late forties. There will be a serious life-threatening event, which begins with the letter C, but don't worry. You will survive."

At this point, my thoughts were racing, as I wasn't exactly prepared for bad news about my health. I could only think about a *disease* that could start with C. Sheepishly, I asked, "Is it cancer?"

He started to shake his head slowly from side to side. "No, it's not cancer".

Before I could name another disease (although at the time I couldn't think of anything else) he said, "There will be a misdiagnosis. It will take several more years for you to recover, but again you will survive." Unprompted by me, he added, "In your mid fifties, you will go on and be most well known for your writings!"

As our reading came to an end, I didn't really know what to think. I couldn't understand how I was feeling, mostly because I didn't want any of the bad things said to be true; so I simply shrugged it off as an interesting experience. Even many years later, I can say that I didn't let that reading influence any part of my journey, especially when I fell in love with my first husband, Ted, or when I was contemplating my second marriage to Terry. In other words, I didn't think I should *not* marry Ted or Terry because some years earlier I had been forewarned. Besides, at twenty-one, I thought I was pretty invincible. My late forties were still a whole lifetime away.

But if the thing starting with C wasn't cancer, I had no idea what else it could be. Plus—known for my writings? I wasn't interested in writing. I was just beginning to think about careers, and that didn't really give me an "A-ha!" moment.

Today, remembering that reading is more than a little interesting. Was it coincidence or fate that I had been married twice by the age of thirty-seven, or that the serious, life-threatening event that started with C and would cause my medical problems, was not cancer but a plane crash when I was forty-seven? I most definitely had many injuries, and I was misdiagnosed with a broken left foot that prolonged my recovery by a couple of years—just like the medium had forewarned all those years ago.

Believe me, too: when the crash occurred, I was instantly reminded of that reading, and became at least curious about the idea of writing about my experience. I find it also interesting, that I can remember nothing else of what he said, but remembered verbatim his predictions about my future. I have written my story. This isn't an advice book or a how to book, but if I may; one small piece of advice would be to surrender, because your life is already written for you ... by you.

> *"Re-examine all you have been told. Dismiss what insults your soul."*
>
> —*Walt Whitman*

Part One: The Early Years

Chapter One—A Change of Destiny

On January 21, 2006, when I was forty-seven years old, my whole "perfect princess" world unexpectedly and instantly changed forever.

Terry, my husband of twelve-and- half-years, and I had just spent four romantic days at the Wickaninnish Inn, a luxury spa and resort in Tofino, on Vancouver Island. We reluctantly boarded the single-engine commuter plane that would take us back to Vancouver, and back to reality. I say reluctantly only because these times together are what I craved for most in my marriage to Terry. Like many of us on the fast track, our lives were full and busy. Getting Terry alone for what I call connection time was a rarity, so when I could, I treasured it all that much more.

A few minutes into the flight, I pulled James Frey's novel, *A Million Little Pieces*, out of my purse, thinking I would read for a while. Instead, I kept thinking back on that morning. I was so pleased with myself, because I had planned this trip some months ago, and had finally fulfilled a desire of mine: to share a romantic couple's massage with my husband. The four days were magical and perfect. I felt connected. The icing on the cake for me was that Terry enjoyed it, too!

Suddenly—*bang!* As I watched in horror, the single propeller at the front of the plane slowly wound down to a dead halt! The sound of the engine had stopped, leaving it now eerily silent in the small plane. The seven passengers were suddenly stunned into silence; the only voice I heard was the pilot's as he called his maydays to the air-traffic controller back at the tower.

We all looked around at each other on full alert. Our new reality was that we were now trapped in a plane with no power, approximately 9,000 feet over the Pacific Ocean. Now what? Surely there was an emergency button, or something else the pilot could activate? My mind couldn't quite fully comprehend how dire our situation was, but somehow my body knew. My stomach did a few flips and my armpits were now sweating; I felt very anxious and fearful.

Terry had moved to sit upright on the edge of his seat, quietly surveying the situation from his vantage point, which was right behind the cockpit. Perhaps he was feeling (and I'm only guessing now, because we exchanged no words) that he might be experiencing something similar to what the passengers felt on the flights on 9/11 in 2001, when some citizens decided they had to do something to get their planes to safety. Instead, as Terry's look went from startled awareness to resignation, he finally turned to me, shaking his head, and said very clearly, "This doesn't look very good."

As I looked into his eyes, I was shocked and confused when another pair of round, wide-set, blue eyes, with distinct wrinkles around them, superimposed themselves over Terry's for several seconds! I locked onto his gaze and stared in disbelief as a stranger's eyes continued to stare out at me. *What could this possibly mean, especially at a time like this?* I thought.

As I looked behind me at the other passengers I became aware that everyone was in what appeared to be their own state of utter disbelief and horror. Still, no one overtly panicked. We all seemed to come to the realization that there was no way out of this predicament;

we could do nothing but wait for the inevitable. We were going down! Where? I'm guessing not even the pilot knew for certain.

At some point, an unusual calmness permeated the air. I know I was doing my own life review, and it appeared Terry was as well. He seemed to strike the pose of Rodin's famous *Thinker*: chin in hand in sober meditation, battling a powerful internal struggle. What flashed before me, besides my life up until that point, was the fact that I saw how I'd been led to something this immense, this critical, to force me to take a new direction in my life. Somehow I knew I would survive. Moreover, I sensed that Terry knew that these were his last moments on Earth. What the other passengers were thinking, I wouldn't know because no one really said much. However, this much was for sure: all of us cocooned in that small plane had no control over our destinies anymore.

As the pilot and the air traffic controllers desperately tried to determine the best course of action, the plane glided silently through the air, all the while losing altitude and speed. It was just as bleak outside as it was inside the plane. Clouds and rain surrounded us. We had little to no visual connection to the ground toward which we were free falling, and I'm only guessing now, at several hundred miles per hour. Completely helpless, I turned inward and started to pray like I have never prayed before.

A few moments later, although I was lost in my own thoughts, my attention turned back to the pilot. After some discussion with the tower, he unexpectedly made a sharp right-hand turn back toward the airport in Tofino. The turn felt like being in a car that was going very fast around a corner; an unexpected and sudden hold-onto-your-seats type of turn. My stomach flipped upside down once again and I started to pray harder. *This isn't a seaplane,* I thought. *Please, don't try to do an ocean landing.*

I had a sudden vision of the airplane crash that had killed John Kennedy, Jr., his wife, Carolyn Bessette-Kennedy, and her sister. *Oh, please, God, turn this plane toward the mountains.* After only a few moments and some more urgent communications, the pilot once again abruptly turned the plane; we were now heading south, toward land. I was simply praying that the pilot knew where he was going and wondering how much experience this young man had. Not to sound facetious, but I hoped they practiced emergency landings like this in flight school.

I learned later that when the pilot turned abruptly he was trying to get out of the cloud to get a visual connection to the ground. Unfortunately, we lost valuable gliding distance and could not make it to a logging road or the nearest airport, which was located on the other side of the island in Port Alberni.

The only communication between the passengers and the young pilot occurred just moments before we crashed, when he indicated to us all to fasten our seat belts as tight as we could and to get ready for the impending impact. As if anyone could ever be ready for that!

To make matters worse, there were two little children on board. They were crying and obviously very unsure of what was going on. Their mom was doing her best to comfort them and buckle them up. Unfortunately, an eighteen-month-old and a three-year-old child can't really be strapped into an adult seat very well. (Later, an investigation resulted in a recommendation by the Transportation Safety Board that, just like a child seat in a car is mandatory, a child seat in a plane would also be beneficial for circumstances like these. Otherwise, they are like little torpedoes upon impact).

By now, the clouds had parted and there was a momentary glimpse of hope in the form of sunshine that now seemingly illuminated our way. For fifteen terrifying minutes we flew into uncertainty. I don't know which was worse: being able to see what we were going to hit, or not. However, from where I was sitting, I could now see the forest and sense that the pilot was losing control of the plane. I still thought about my life and what had just happened with Terry's eyes and what could that mean?

I turned my thoughts to Terry and I and really just surrendered. He had always been my knight in shining armor; he had always been in charge, able to handle any difficult situation. In the end, dread set in as I realized that Terry was not going to be able to get us out of this situation—not this time.

Terry and I turned to each other and mouthed, *"I love you."* In one final loving gesture, Terry motioned to me to get into the tucked position for impact, which I did. We then turned away to face our own fates. Minutes later, shortly after 2:00 P.M., the Cessna 208 Caravan clipped the tops of some trees and then dove nose-first at a sixty-degree angle into a clear-cut section of a remote forest on Vancouver Island, some ten kilometers short of the Port Alberni airport. And everything went black.

Chapter Two—My Hole-in-One Duck Dream

"In order to understand where you are going,
You need to understand where you have come from."
—*Maya Angelou*

One thing I know for sure is that I am a survivor. Why I got a second chance at life is no longer a mystery to me, but it took surviving this plane crash and having a near death experience for me to really hear what my soul was lovingly trying to say to me, because up until this point in my life, I hadn't really been listening. I had some unfinished work to do.

I have a simple reason for sharing my story: I want to inspire those who have had a major accident or other life-altering event in their own lives, like death of a loved one, divorce or unexpected job loss, to see it as a gift instead of a tragedy. Our reactions to life-altering events are what make us either victims or victors in life. There are no accidents, and there are no exceptions. I also want to share my spiritual journey and transformation from a quasi-nonbeliever to someone with 'knowingness' that I am one with my source, which I call God.

On the surface my story is about surviving the plane crash; but the real story or most inspirational part is the story that lies beneath.

The crash and heroics required getting the survivors off the mountain is certainly captivating; however, this was my life; not a sensational news story that is forgotten days later. The triumph for me would be to share the real human part of the story. How many lives were significantly affected forever? More importantly, it was realizing that it was the catalyst to make me see some truths in my life, that for up until the actual accident, I failed to acknowledge. Was my life an illusion up until then?

My happiness, peace, health, and contentment rest squarely on my shoulders and my shoulders alone. I discovered my true purpose in life had nothing to do with any of the material things I acquired, places I'd been, or titles to which I aspired. However, for most of my life, I was too afraid to examine it from the inside or even contemplate getting off the fast track; I wore a mask that covered many perceived blemishes. When I was finally stripped of all my masks, not only in the hospital settings but also in the legal dramas that ensued, I saw nothing but love and beauty reflecting back in the mirror. I can now say I love myself unconditionally ... scars and all! Finding that acceptance was *not* instantaneous, but believe me, the process was well worth the effort.

Each step along the way of recovery beautifully laid out for me some karmic lessons I needed to learn and address in this lifetime. During the excavation process, I uncovered some truths, both positive and negative, that had held me back from my true purpose in life. My soul kept trying to tell me, "Love more; want less; simplify your life."

I found a great deal of comfort in reading about other people's similar tragedies during my long recovery. Misery must truly love company! I had never experienced quite so much misery all at once. I found myself particularly motivated by the true story, *Ninety Minutes in Heaven,* co-written by Don Piper with Cecil Murphey. I was relating to his multiple injuries to his legs and strenuous torture he had to go to just to be able to walk again. I was very intrigued by his story of crossing over for ninety minutes and then coming back to life to discover his true purpose.

The other truly inspiring story was by Dr. Jill Bolte Taylor, Ph.D., author of *My Stroke of Insight,* a brain scientist in real life; whose own stroke at the age of thirty-seven, made her realize the connection between her mind, and her spirit and that peace or nirvana are never more than a thought away. She spent eight long years recovering from not being able to walk, talk, read, write or recall her life to finally being able to teach once again. Her whole purpose changed in that moment she had her stroke. The connection and the reality that we are more than just our bodies, we are spirit encapsulated in human form and we are all connected inspired her to get better.

The list goes on, but suffice to say, I was inspired to think, *if they can do it, I can too! I knew I was given a second chance at life and that there must be a reason for all this. I simply had no idea what that was yet. Eventually I would be able to silence my mind and be able to really listen to why I was here and why I survived.*

One day in the third year of my recovery, as I continued to write and reflect on my life, I had a vivid dream—a message from my soul or spirit guides. In my dream, I was a ten-year-old girl again. I was standing on a tee box with a golf club in my hand. A group of older ladies surrounded the green with pens and notepads, ready to record my every stroke. They demanded that I hit the ball right that instant. Instead, I just wanted to play with the ducks waddling near by. After quite some time of trying to ignore their demands, I started to get annoyed. They continued to harass me, calling, "Go ahead and just hit the ball."

A few minutes of frustration and much taunting later, I stood up and shouted angrily, "All right, already!" I teed up the ball, took one effortless swing, and watched as it soared perfectly toward the hole, bounced once, and went in!

I threw down the club and said, rather defiantly "Are you satisfied now?" Then I went back to playing with the ducks.

In her book *Dream Yourself Awake*, Darlene Montgomery, a well-known author and speaker on dreams, states, "Dreams are not random and jumbled images, but rather important and meaningful road maps winding through the fabric of our life, showing us possibilities that remind us of our higher purpose." This inspired me to reexamine my childhood and my roots in more depth. I needed to put some closure, once and for all, to the disappointments, anger, resentments, and frustrations I had silently carried with me well past my childhood and into my adult hood. These emotional pains had begun manifesting in my body as physical discomfort long before the plane crash. For all of my life I had kept these negative emotions neatly tucked inside, never daring to admit to them or express them. I held onto them like a badge of honor. But as I began to excavate my life during my recovery, I finally started to make the connection as to why I had been in the accident—or, better expressed, why I survived it.

Many limiting subconscious beliefs were holding me back from my true potential and thus real happiness. These beliefs were *not* true, but because they wound so deeply into my life, almost as though they existed on a cellular level in my own DNA, and manifested themselves on a subconscious level, I wasn't making any connections as to how I was feeling and what might be holding me back. According to Bruce Lipton, co-author of *Spontaneous Evolution* and an internationally recognized authority in bridging science and spirit and a leading voice in new biology, 95 percent of our thoughts come from the subconscious.

The biology of our bodies can be urged toward health and wellness by what we think and say. Our beliefs are just thoughts we keep telling ourselves over and over again. And if 95 percent of those thoughts are subconscious, meaning they *are* hard-wired into the very DNA that makes up the biology of our bodies, then in order to change our wellness, we need to change those limiting beliefs. In simple terms, we really are what we think about—even from our past lives. Often, because they are subconscious, we continue to get the same results and attract the same people and situations into our life over repeated existences.

Until and unless I was willing to look inside and change my limiting and negative beliefs, I would stay stuck in circumstances that would play out not only this lifetime, but also possibly every lifetime still to come. These are my lessons I came here to learn. This time, however, God wasn't whispering nor nudging me anymore. It took the plane crash to show me all the connections and make me realize this.

As the saying goes, I can't change what I won't acknowledge.

I knew exactly the connection and the meaning of this duck dream. And that takes me back to the beginning of my childhood … and thus the early years of my story.

Chapter Three—The Performance Begins

Many spiritual teachers have proclaimed that you actually choose your parents before you're born. I understood that truth long ago; unfortunately, I didn't appreciate the full extent of its meaning until I could look back over my life. Once I left my parents' home and got onto the fast track of life, I never took the time to look back. Getting off that fast track never even occurred to me. I only knew one direction and one speed – straight ahead and fast.

It was only during the months of recovery that I came to understand I had chosen the most perfect parents possible for me to become the person I am today. Also, every misstep in my life had brought me to a place where the changes I would need to make in order to be authentically empowered and happy became as plain as the nose on my face.

The review of my life, both moments before we crashed and then after, were just part of my journey that I needed to take in order for me to realize this one thing that I had been searching for all of my life. I know now that the messages from God eventually went from whispers to very strong nudges to an absolute whack over the head for me to see the beauty in this truth.

I was born and named Barbara Jill Badger on April 10, 1958, at the General Hospital in Winnipeg, Manitoba. Barbara was the name of my mom's best friend growing up. She preferred the name Jill; however, she liked the sound of "Barbara Jill" better than "Jill Barbara." Everyone therefore called me by my middle name; sometimes my close friends call me "Jilly." I answer to both.

I was the baby and the only girl in the family. As a teen I learned that my mom had had a miscarriage between my middle brother and me. My mom was thirty-two and my dad was twenty-nine when I was born. Back then, thirty-two was considered very late for a woman to still be having babies. So was I really wanted or was I an accident? Because I was a girl, how would my birth affect the family dynamics?

There are hundreds of photos of Rick, their first-born boy; fewer of Steve, the middle boy; and shockingly few of me. Me ... the only girl and the cutest of all! Occasionally I go through the family albums and see pictures of myself on the day I was born, then again as a toddler just learning to take my first steps, and then one picture where I appear to be about four or five, posing with pigtails and purse in hand.

My parents would line us three kids up either on the front steps or in front of the family car for our yearly family picture, which included Tiger, our dog, Rarely were there pictures of just me. Fortunately from then on the pictures of just of me were the usual school pictures. I guess by the time the third child comes along, the cuteness and novelty wears off, as does the concomitant photography. Still, the lack of pictures doesn't erase my childhood memories, despite the obvious gaps in time. Instead, I think it only proves that my parents were really busy raising three very active children.

We moved into our brand-new two-story, four-bedroom house in the spring of 1962. The house was on Doran Bay, in St. James Assiniboine. As in most new subdivisions, the families were young; all the parents were looking for quiet, friendly streets for their family to grow and thrive. The landscape had a good scattering of new homes with a lot of wide-open fields in between—perfect places to play and just be kids.

In those days nobody locked the doors, especially during the day. Perhaps at night when we were all tucked in bed, my dad would have locked the front door, but there was never any threat of danger in not doing so. While we may have been the start of the latchkey generation because no parent awaited us when we got home from school, we never felt any fear. We would just go home and either do homework, watch TV, or play outside.

The neighborhood fostered a great sense of community; we enjoyed a simple, happy life there. My family still thinks fondly of our time on Doran Bay, for everybody kind of pulled together to help one another. Whether it was for the building of fences, the laying of backyard sod, running to the store for milk, or babysitting for a few minutes while one mom ran an errand, neighbor helped neighbor. Somehow, in our little community, we were still connected to such worldly events as man landing on the moon. In fact, it was our black-and-white TV with rabbit ears that we brought outside so all the neighbors could gather round; together we heard Neil Armstrong, all the way out there on the moon, say, "One small step for man, one giant leap for mankind!" We all felt such great sense of triumph.

Before I turned six, my mom was a stay-at-home mom, but she returned to full time work once I started the first grade. She worked the late shift (four P.M. to midnight) as a tele-typist at the local newspaper, the *Winnipeg Free Press*. Back in the early '60s, people considered such action fairly nontraditional. Most of my friend's mothers stayed home, so they were always around to handle any childhood crisis: lost winter mittens, skinned knees, hurt feelings, and many more unforeseen events. As the decade wore on, a few more mothers did start to work at least part-time, but my mom was one of the few exceptions that worked full time.

Often, dinnertime did not go well. Since Mom worked and thus absent for dinnertime, my dad was left cooking and feeding us three kids. In reality, Mom would have everything prepared in advance and all Dad had to do was to reheat the food—but still, there was almost always some drama, usually centering on our picky eating habits. We did not like being forced to eat our vegetables. Dad would threaten us by hurling plastic dishes in the vicinity of our heads in response. My brothers and I got very good at ducking. I know my dad never aimed to hit us, but it scared me and made eating as a family a very tense time. We would have to sit at the dinner table until we finished every last morsel. Sometimes we managed, but when we really didn't like the food, we'd just sit there for hours. Finally, we were excused. Thankfully, Tiger was an eager and easy receptacle for all unwanted food. If Tiger wasn't around, Steve used to stuff the food in his pockets and go visit the bathroom. At least he was cleverer than I. Still, it made dinnertimes not exactly like those on *Leave it to Beaver*!

I started to equate food with goodness or badness. My thinking was that if I wanted to be perfect, which I thought was necessary to get my dad's approval and to keep him in a good mood, I would have to learn to control all foods that went into my mouth. To this day, I associate the word "bad" with a chocolate-chip cookie, whereas most people might say "delicious" or some other positive word association. It took a lot of reprogramming for me to learn to enjoy food and not to label it so harshly. I still work on it almost every day.

Cleary, my mom Gerry was not really the homemaker type. Over the years she had her moments of domestic bliss, but I think she preferred and enjoyed the fact that she could get dressed up in nice clothes, have her hair done, put on make-up, and be a part of the new working class of women. While she was no woman's libber, she had other financial motivations that contributed to her decision.

Both my parents grew up in the Depression era and achieved only a high school education. My dad chose to enter the accounting field, and while one-income families were quite normal in those days, it

16

became obvious that we needed a second salary for my parents to afford three kids and a mortgage and still the lifestyle they dreamed of attaining. We were comfortable and decidedly middle class, but striving for more was probably our family's attempt to keep up with the Joneses. I never knew differently, and I never felt deprived.

Rhonda McFarlane was my best friend from grades one through six. Her mom became my surrogate mother, the one who administered the cookies and the love after school, or helped me with any major calamity in my life that happened during my mom's absence. Rhonda and I were inseparable during those years; it nearly broke my heart when their family was transferred to Regina at the end of our sixth grade year.

Rhonda and I had so many things in common. We both had two brothers and blonde hair; we were also both very smart. There were differences too, of course: her brothers were younger than she was, while mine were three and six years older. Also, she wasn't interested in sports, nor was she terribly athletic—but I certainly was!

I was probably more of a tomboy than Rhonda, but only because I was athletic, not because I didn't like "girl things" in some way. My girly-girl persona existed just beneath the surface, waiting to be expressed; my athleticism simply overshadowed it. That athleticism seemed to light up my dad—and thus me, because I adored my dad. I was a daddy's girl when I was young. My brothers were okay at sports, but for some reason, I was the one who was chosen to fulfill my dad's fading dreams of ever being a sports star. In my Dad's youth, he was athletic and excelled in and competed at baseball, golf and gymnastics. In those days, if you didn't have a higher education, you were expected to get married and have a family. The responsibility of family overtook your individual aspirations, especially if they lay in the sports world.

Steve and I were the blonde poster children of the family. In fact, until at least grades two or three we were mistaken for twins, despite that fact that he was three years older than I. In those days, I braided my pigtails and wore color-coordinated grosgrain or velvet ribbons to match my many outfits. In fact, for much of grade school, my dad cut our hair. I think my brothers got the short end of the stick; at least I could just trim my bangs and tie the rest back into pigtails. My brothers, however, had to endure the one-stop buzz cut, or in later years, the ever-popular bowl cut. Home haircut bangs were never straight! But my dad was just being thrifty.

Steven also got all my oldest brother's hand me downs. I, however, always got new clothes. While my mom didn't sew, she did love to knit, and she made some incredibly beautiful knit outfits for me. I remember having different ballerina shoes to match each of my outfits when I was about eight or nine: purple, pink, gold, and black. I was definitely spoiled when it came to clothes. My mom took pride in making sure that I was always in fashion. I never objected; in fact, I cultivated an identity of being the girl who was perfectly put together. I was different. I know I wouldn't have understood that back then, but I can't help but wonder now as a grown adult, if my desire to always look perfectly presented started back then.

There were no school buses in the early years. We kids walked or ran to school in our neighborhood groups, even in the dead of winter. Only on very rare occasions would school be completely cancelled for the day due to freezing temperatures or major snowstorms. I remember the pain of removing my winter snow boots, the inevitable tears while I waited for my frozen toes and fingers to thaw. Somehow, though, the process was comforting, because now I was safe and warm in the classroom.

Grade school was academically easy for me. I was always the eager student, sitting in the front of the class waving desperately for the teacher to call on me. I got glasses in grade one, so I *had* to sit close to the front, just to see the board. I didn't want to miss anything. Every year my myopia got worse, and every year, my mom and dad had to buy me new glasses. Having coke-bottle-thick glasses by my teenage years didn't help my self-esteem.

Regardless of that, my childhood was fairly normal. I was a willing straight-A student who made friends easily. The comments from my teachers were always along the lines of, "It is a pleasure to have Jill in our classroom. She is an excellent student, learns easily, and participates well in class." The parent-teacher meetings were never a problem for my mom or dad. As the years passed, only my mom would go; my dad preferred playing bridge in the evenings to hearing what he already knew. It was true: I always had glowing report cards.

Despite my desire to be a good student, I started to test my boundaries as early as grade three. I was caught talking while the teacher was talking—a definite no-no! My punishment was to stand at the back of the room with my arms out to my sides for what seemed like a very long time. This humiliated and embarrassed me, so I never once talked out in class again. Being sent to the principal's office for the strap was a frightening thought that kept me toeing the line all throughout grade school.

I was very sensitive as a small girl, though, and no wonder—I was always being picked on. Around the time I got in trouble for talking, other children began to focus their energies on making me miserable. A certain group of boys often chased me home. During recess, kids picked on and bullied me, but the teachers supervising did little, if nothing, to stop this. They figured it was just kids being kids.

I didn't really even know it was called bullying, because I had two older brothers who did the exact same thing to me at home. In a way, I was used to it. Even in later years at family gatherings, my brothers would enjoy recounting how they used to torment me while I was sleeping. They used to sneak into my bedroom after I fell asleep and tickle my nose with a pink feather pen I used to have on my desk—all unbeknownst to my parents, who of course would have stopped it. This form of entertainment kept them occupied for hours.

Luckily, unlike at school, when it got too bad at home, I jut had to start screaming and my dad would come running with the vacuum hose. He used the hose as a threat if my brothers didn't stop doing whatever I was accusing them of doing. My mom's way to comfort me was to try and assure me the boys who chased me home just liked me, or that the girls who called me names actually envied me. There was no explanation for why my brothers liked to bully me, other than they did and could because I was the youngest.

I never fought back; I was far too much a good girl to risk doing anything to call more attention to myself. Instead, I silently suffered the ridicule despite learning the little ditty, "Sticks and stones may break my bones, but names will never hurt me." I didn't know that eventually my self-esteem would be stunted by this continual bullying behavior.

The famous gumdrop caper laid the groundwork for my fear of telling the truth. My mom was planning on making a new gumdrop cookie recipe and had put the package of gumdrops in the hiding place for all things off-limits to us kids –in the cupboard above the stove. Curiosity and impatience got the better of me, so one day; I decided I couldn't wait for the cookies to be made. Like a big girl, I climbed on a chair, retrieved the gumdrops and ate the whole bag. Everything appeared to have gone smoothly; I did it all by myself, without having to ask, tell, or share with my brothers! Unfortunately, a few days later, I found myself in a line-up with my two brothers being interrogated by Dad as to who ate the gumdrops. All three kids denied it, which prolonged the interrogation. Finally, after realizing my brothers weren't going to fess up, I had to tell the truth. I don't remember my punishment from my parents, but for the rest of my life, my personal punishment was replayed every single time my brothers once again retorted with laughter over the gumdrop caper.

In grade six, things turned around a little for me because one particular boy, who had a crush on me, began following me like a puppy dog, always asking to carry my books. He was like my personal assistant and the start of the persona of what eventually I would be labeled as "a princess." He and I lived at opposite ends of the community so I only let him carry my books on the days I went to my piano lesson, which were conveniently close to where he lived. On other days, even though he earnestly wanted to, I said no. I was capable of carrying my own books.

Since I was just entering puberty, I was embarrassed and confused by this sort of positive attention. The boy wasn't exactly a nerd, nor was he considered a really cool kid—but he was cool enough for me. He was one of the few who were nice to me, besides Rhonda.

Life wasn't always difficult. I loved telling my mom what I had learned that day in school; for most of my grade school years, she would just marvel at how well I did. I was devastated if I missed one or two points on a spelling quiz. Mom just said, "Honey, you got all the others right; don't worry about the one or two you missed." As a budding pint-sized perfectionist, such errors were devastating. Even then, I always thought it was odd how my own mother would marvel at me. She mused, "Jill, I was never as smart as you. I never liked to get up in front of the class, nor was I ever the first one chosen when it came to games or sports." Looking back, I can see I was more of an inspiration to my mom than she was ever capable of being for me.

Until I was about ten, most of my summers were spent playing kick-the-can, dodge ball, or hide and seek. We used the telephone pole conveniently located in our front yard as the starting point for many games that all the neighborhood kids joined. "Play" is the operative word here, because that is what I remember the most of my early childhood years: we just got to play and run outside all day long. We didn't stop until one of our moms yelled, "Dinner!" That call was the signal that we all had to obey, and we'd troop off home to eat. But soon after our dinner, we'd all gather again and resume our games.

The four seasons were the best part of growing up in Winnipeg, because every three months, the climate changed quite dramatically. There was always something to look forward to. Winnipeg, being just north of the forty-ninth parallel, had long, hot, sticky, mosquito-infested summers. Often, the highlight of a summer evening was to sit as a family and watch the thunderstorms roll in.

Spring saw the winter's snow melt, creating huge puddles just begging us to jump into them with glee. Rubber boots replaced our heavy winter boots. There was always a familiar fresh spring smell in the air; you knew, finally, the winter was coming to an end. Autumns were highlighted by the return to school and the excitement of getting new books and clothes, along with the enjoyment and familiarity of the school routine. Now the familiar smell was musty, as the furnace clanked on in the early mornings to wake us up and blow the dust around a bit.

Finally, winters were long, cold, and dark—my favorite time to hibernate. What kid from the prairies didn't learn the hard way not to put his or her tongue on anything steel? It was a rite of passage; once you made that mistake, you never did it again!

While I never took skating lessons, I still tried to emulate the grace of the figure skaters I saw on TV, like Peggy Fleming. Fifteen minutes was usually about all we could endure before our frozen fingers and toes forced us from the outdoor skating rink into the warmth of the indoor community center. Occasionally we would be given a quarter so we could buy candy from the canteen. I always bought my favorites: black licorice, gummy bears, or strawberry candies.

Sometime during grades two to five, I took tap-dancing and baton-twirling lessons. I loved being on stage and particularly loved to dance. I don't know the real reason my dance lessons stopped; I hope it wasn't because of the cost of the costumes. Mom would have wanted me to have the *right* costume, but if she couldn't make it and we couldn't afford it, then how was I going to be able to continue dancing? Whatever the reason, my dance lessons stopped suddenly in grade five or six, taking my dream of becoming a dancer with them.

Television didn't play a central role in our lives, at least not in the summer when we could play outside. We watched only after school or on the weekends, when we would gather at the foot of our parent's bed. Friday was fudge night; Saturday was popcorn night and Sunday was pie night. Desserts and other sugary treats were a definite hit in our family. I also remember a lot of fighting around who controlled the TV. In those days you had to get up and change the channel. As the youngest and the only girl, I lost the contest a lot.

By then, I had also taken up piano lessons, as had my brother Steve. I never enjoyed having to practice the piano for hours on end each week. Unfortunately, my parents forced—I mean, *encouraged*—Steve and me to perform any time their friends visited. Steve was clearly more musically inclined than I was, which discouraged me because I never liked being second in anything. Eventually I quit. I had other things to conquer.

I took a clue from my natural athletic ability and plunged headlong into baseball and eventually golf, with which I had a love/hate relationship as a child—and, in fact, for most of my early adult years. Around the age of ten, my carefree life in the summers went from playing outside with my friends to being carted off to a golf course and literally dropped there all day long. My dad in particular liked to play golf and thought this would be a good family thing to do. I know my parents figured that if they could keep us kids busy, we wouldn't get into trouble. In those days, that decision probably wasn't all that bad, because what real trouble could we get into on a private golf course? I can certainly think of worse scenarios; that said, I was still a young girl who wanted to be with her girl friends, not her brothers.

There was never any discussion of whether or not I would like to play golf; it was decided for me, and in order not to anger my dad, I simply went along. I felt very controlled as a young girl. To make matters worse, every month after the country club food bill would come in, my dad would give us all a stern lecture (really, more like definite ranting and raving) about spending on food. What did they expect? We were growing kids, left to play golf all day long, and naturally we got hungry. My reaction was to eat less, while my brother Steve kept on ordering chocolate milkshakes, whistle dogs, and French fries. He never seemed to worry about my dad's monthly ranting, but I sure did.

I hated every moment of my early golfing years and recall spending most of the time crying. Not only were there not any other girls to play with, I had to play with teenage boys and or with my bullying brothers. I could barely hit that little white ball, and the game had so many *stupid* rules!

In the scant array of pictures of my childhood, there is one that perfectly conveys my feelings about golf. The scowl on my face reflects my complete lack of joy despite my mom's best effort to make that day special and fun for Steve and me. She too never really liked to play 18 holes of golf, but she did enjoy the socializing with the women from the Country Club.

But still, an eight-hour workday at the course (my mom would drop us off in the morning and my dad would pick us up after work) was very long for any little girl. It was even worse on days when, after heading home for supper, Dad would then proceed back out to the course to partake in a sport he loved. He had to be very patient with me, for I did not make it any fun. I acted out in the only way I knew how and that was to cry and complain. On those mosquito-infested, hot, sticky evenings, with three young kids to drag around a golf course, he lovingly did his best!

During the day, we were only allowed on the actual golf course at certain times and usually only with adult supervision until we got a little better and a little older. These ladies would literally stand beside you and record in their notebook every single swing (including the whiffs) you took. We spent a lot of time on the putting green and the practice range, where we would make up our own games. Of course, once out on the course, we followed the rules to a letter. There was no cheating allowed.

Despite my frustration, I eventually learned to cope by performing. I equated my performance success with attention from my dad. When I performed well, I thought he loved me. When I didn't perform quite so well, I felt him withdraw his attention and, I assumed, his love.

Fortunately, as I got older, a few girls did take up the sport and I could play with them. I began entering tournaments and either winning outright or at least placing. Although I was labeled competitive, I never really felt that way. It was just a way to conform and stay alive, especially around my brothers.

But because I was now entering some tournaments, I had to learn to put on my game face and be something that I felt deep down I was not. I would always be sick to my stomach before a tournament, having difficulty eating the days before and after. I was always uncomfortable in competitive situations, and soon this performance anxiety spilled over to other areas of my life. I learned to survive by sucking it up and hiding my true feelings. This is when I learned to put on one of my many masks, trying to be perfect to be loved.

Chapter Four—The Ghosts of Christmas Past

Christmas was always joyous time around the Badger house, until the concept of a bleak Christmas was introduced. I was around eight when I learned the truth about Santa. Maybe it was the frenzy into which the schools whipped the children, with the excitement of the Christmas school plays coupled with the overload of sugar, that made my dad feel like he had to bring it down a notch or two. For whatever reason, he found a way to dampen the fun the rest of the family anticipated.

My dad's company gave out bonuses in January, and whether he knew in advance if he was getting a bonus or not, he always told us it would be a cash-strapped holiday. Not until well into the New Year did he then announce that in fact he did get some sort of sizable bonus. This definitely had a negative effect on my gift-giving thoughts for at least the next several years to come.

Maybe Dad just felt the strain of the added expenses and this was his way of helping us to feel grateful for what we did have? He would later recall that when he was young he got only one Christmas present each year, while his sister got several. My brothers' recollection to this day is that I got more presents than they ever did. My mom assured us she was always fair and we always got the exact same number of presents.

Fortunately, Mom was the one in charge of the entire running of the household and all Christmas gift buying. Despite my dad's comments, she would see to it that each of us kids got at least two or three presents from Santa, plus a stocking filled with Christmas treats! We also received presents from our relatives, and while we didn't have a large extended family, we were in no way shortchanged when it came to receiving presents on Christmas morning.

My favorite parts of Christmas were decorating the tree and eating my mom's lemon tarts. Well, and also her short bread cookies, her famous snowballs, and yes, the caramel candies—all were delights. She did like to bake, and in later years I learned all of my culinary skills from her. Baking became synonymous with love to me.

In those days, we would buy a real tree down at the local shopping mall parking lot. I don't know if it was intentional, but somehow, our Christmas trees were always just one, maybe two grades above a Charlie Brown-esque, scraggly, sad Christmas tree. Still, every year we would excitedly drag out the box of decorations from the basement and have at it. I always secretly wanted to be in charge, but I did have two older brothers to whom I had to acquiesce, as well a father who liked to direct from his chair while refereeing us kids. I loved the glitter and all the lights. This must have been the start of my penchant for design!

Even as the years wore on, the threat of bleakness died down (my dad changed companies), and the real tree morphed into a convenient fake one, Christmas morning was always special and somewhat overdone, even excessive. My brother Steve may have exhibited the most excitement: he would have already opened his stocking and consumed most of his candy by the time he barged into my room at six A.M. to see what I got. Interestingly, not much has changed even now.

Christmas morning was also the only day that my dad chose to sleep in. The other 364 days of the year, he would be up at the crack of dawn, even on weekends; but on Christmas, we couldn't start opening our big presents until Dad said so, which was not until around 8:30 or 9:00. My mom would have been up until all hours on Christmas Eve, lovingly wrapping each of our presents. I know she got a lot of personal satisfaction from preparing Christmas for her family. She did her best to make it special for all of us, even though my dad did his best to play Scrooge. Thinking back on it, I believe he secretly enjoyed the holiday; only he wasn't comfortable expressing his true feelings. In fact, my dad has always been generous with his money; he never had a lot, but what he did have, he was happy to give to his kids.

Every other year, our family would go to my Aunt Jerry and Uncle Gordon's house for the traditional turkey and trimmings. My mom probably enjoyed it the most, because she finally got a day off from cooking. We kids looked forward to it because at our aunt's house we got to have the treats that were usually forbidden at home. A lot of my memories include feeling ill by the end of Christmas Day, or my brother Steve throwing up on the way home from too much sugar. You'd think we'd learn, but we didn't! Maybe we felt it just wasn't Christmas unless we all got sick.

My uncle had the job of constantly refilling our tiny juice glasses. I don't think he realized we could consume far more than the small glasses he attempted to use to satisfy our thirst. He spent his entire Christmas dinner bouncing up every few seconds to keep us all happy. While we did our best to behave, we were too wired to be able to control our excitement. I'm sure they were glad it was only every other year that we came for holiday dinner!

When the meal ended, the fun continued as we learned to play poker with real poker chips that we cashed in at the end of the evening for real money. I would team up with my favorite uncle and together we would learn to play all kinds of card games. I seem to recall winning a lot, but my parents made sure that if and when I did lose, I had to lose my money as well.

"Hokey-pokey-diddly-okey!" said my aunt every time she would either roll the dice or take a card. She was a natural winner, which used to annoy my dad to no end.

Finally, around 8:00 P.M., my dad would head outside to try to start the inevitably frozen car. The temperatures around that time of year often dipped to thirty degrees below. Even though cars back then had block heaters, I don't think there was any way to plug it in. Many years our tires were frozen solid to the point that we would bump our way home among the ruts created by the snowdrifts, sugarplum fairies still dancing in our heads.

The years we didn't go to their house, our family would play host to the relatives. On these occasions, my mother's sister and her husband, Aunt Helen and Uncle Bob, Elsie, my only grandmother, and Aunt Jerry and Uncle Gordon, came over. Bob unfortunately was an alcoholic, so much of the time, I remember my mom protecting me from him. I think he used to want to kiss and hug me, which made me very uncomfortable (not surprisingly). Mom spent a lot of time shielding me whenever my uncle tried to get too close.

As I got older, I noticed that the usual flow of adult drinks that included alcohol was now being controlled around Bob. Some very uncomfortable family moments resulted in his abrupt removal from the invitation list. Eventually he did die of alcohol poisoning, which became the perfect fodder for jokes around alcoholics in our family.

For the most part, we were not a religious group. We never went to church, and certainly the message of Christmas that I recall was more about getting than giving. Only in Sunday school did someone discuss the birth of Jesus. It would even be safe to say that we were either agnostic or atheist—I never really knew the difference between the two, but I did know you didn't talk religion around my family. My mom would say she believed in fate. While I never could get a straight answer from her regarding her beliefs about God, she did make sure that I got some religious instruction. That part wasn't too hard, since many of the families on Doran Bay were either Roman Catholic or Protestant churchgoers, and I was baptized in the United Church of Canada at the age of ten. My brothers were excluded from having to go to church; if I wanted to go, I went alone. Initially, my mom would take me to church when I was very young, but I don't recall her staying for the service. My dad never stepped foot in a church, at least not until I got married the first time.

I recall asking what I thought was an obvious question to my Sunday school teacher and being very quickly shut down. I vaguely recall that I wanted to try to reconcile the differences between what I was learning in science class about how the Earth was formed, and what the Bible said about God making the whole world in seven days! These discrepancies left me very confused. I loved singing songs, I loved saying prayers, and I loved learning, but I did not love being shut down when I asked what I thought was a good question. Suddenly, I stopped going to church. I had a lot of unanswered questions about Jesus and even more about God, but the answers wouldn't come for another forty years or so.

My family just did not fit in with the churchgoing crowd, and I concluded church wasn't for me either. I believe it was less because of any judgments my parents expressed about the other families and their chosen faith, and more what *wasn't* said, that influenced my decision to quit going altogether.

Why did many other families go to church with their kids, but my parents didn't? We were just different. At my best friends' houses, we often said a prayer before we ate, and I liked that sense of calmness around their dinner tables. But I was very tied into what my family believed and stuck to our clan like glue. I didn't even understand the difference between the religious world and the spiritual world until well into my late thirties. The religious world never resonated deeply with me. Eventually, the spiritual teachings that I would come to know rang deep within me, but took many years to surface.

Chapter Five—Weighing In on Image: My Teenage Years

My brothers started teasing me for being pudgy when I was twelve or thirteen. Up until then, I'd been a pretty slender child, and because I was always active and athletic, I never even stopped to think about it. By now, my adolescent figure was starting to take shape, but it was never going to be perfect—at least now not to me, and most definitely not to my brothers.

The truth was that my growth spurt hadn't caught up with my expansion spurt, so as during the early part of puberty, I appeared shorter and heavier. This became perfect fodder for my brothers to tease me about my weight. They also started teasing me about the smallish breasts that had just started developing. To this day, there is one picture of me saluting as a Girl Guide in my uniform, which they liked to laugh at. Still, I can see the joy in my eyes in that photo, and remember how happy I was despite being conscious and uneasy of my new female form.

I became consumed with not being perfect, so I convinced myself to go on a diet. I decided that I would just not eat dinner anymore. After all, I saw my mom on all the popular fad diets, albeit with only short-term success. I was becoming a woman; shouldn't I diet like grown-up women did?

I didn't tell anyone about my plan, particularly my dad, because I feared scolding. My mom might have understood and likely would have tried to discourage me, and I didn't want that. Puberty turned me into a very headstrong girl, and in order for me to feel like I had some control in my life, I was determined to undertake my first diet all by myself.

I grew up with images of my mother standing in front of the mirror that hung on the back of my parent's bedroom door, admonishing herself for her heavy thighs. She would stand with one foot in front of the other, as if to make her hips appear slimmer, and slap at her thighs, all the while exclaiming that she hated them. Sadly, most of my mom's life was spent yo-yo dieting. She never did accept her body as-is. This is an all-too-familiar theme for many women, one that would set the tone for my own unhappiness with my body for many years to come.

Neither of my parents noticed my new dining behavior; it was my little secret. By then, I probably *was* growing taller. I may have lost some weight, but more importantly, as I gained inches, my body slimmed down. I liked what I saw in the mirror, and I really liked the sense of control I felt with my body.

That little secret of mine would rear its ugly head again when I was around twenty-one. It's a wonder it didn't progress into a full-blown eating disorder like anorexia or bulimia, because my feeling as though I were "less than" I should be—a carry-over from my childhood— actually expanded. At that time, I sank into a serious funk over what I was going to do with my life. I felt very unsafe and unsure. Yet, I had no thoughts of ever turning to either of my parents for help.

As I became a young teen, dinnertimes continued to be tense. My palate had expanded, so I wasn't so much opposed to the food as I was to the tension between my parents. This tension centered on my mom's ever changing weight and eating habits. My dad would berate my mom for either what she was eating, or even worse, for what she wasn't eating. He would also taunt her by slathering huge gobs of butter on some bread and saying, "Eat what I eat and you won't be fat."

She couldn't win. For the most part my dad was right, but their way of communicating their differences always shut my mom down emotionally. Out of stubbornness, she just wasn't going to do it his way, whether he was right or wrong. I didn't really understand it then, but after a lifetime of struggling with my weight and thus my image, I certainly see the balance required to be healthy. Moderate exercise, moderate eating, and getting a good night's sleep go a long way toward helping to maintain a healthy body. But back then, I had no idea it could be simple; the disconnect between my emotional body and my physical body had begun.

It's very sad to me that the female body can't be more accepted just for what it is. Why are we never happy with ourselves as we are? Why do we try to change to please others? So many women continue to accept the unrealistic norms set by the fashion and celebrity industries. We are our own worst enemies.

I remember one particular evening. I found my mom crying uncontrollably over the kitchen sink. I tried desperately to comfort her as she begged me not to say anything to my father, because it would only make matters worse. Instead I boiled inside. I was learning to take on my mother's enabling of his bad behavior by *not* speaking my own truth. My mom rarely said anything bad about my dad.

I know there are always two sides of a story, but at least from my perspective, my dad had said something about my mom's weight, which upset her. His way of winning an argument was either to yell louder, or to withdraw completely, either physically or emotionally. It would be fair to say that their arguments rarely ended with mutual respect for their differences. It was more like a "my way or the highway" situation, and the highway had my dad's name on it.

I felt the emotional withdrawal many times, and it could last for weeks at a time. My dad controlled everything and we had to walk on eggshells around him. We never learned to forgive or to apologize. Instead, the tension often ended as if it never even happened. Yet the pain and discomfort could be easily felt, certainly by me and always by my mom.

My family moved from Winnipeg to Vancouver at the end of my grade nine year. Again, my parents decided without any discussion with the kids. My dad had become disillusioned with his company and decided he needed a change. He later told me that he didn't agree with how the bonuses were handled. As the accountant, he could see who was getting what, and he knew the ladies were getting less than their fair share. So kudos to him—but it meant a big upheaval for the family.

Such a move in the middle of my adolescence (I was 15) proved to be very difficult for me. It broke up our family to a family of four because my oldest brother decided to stay in Winnipeg—he had already started university there and wanted to continue. Personally, I had to start grade ten in a new high school with no friends. Another challenge! I know my parents thought it would be easy for me, because I had always gotten along and had made very good friends. But starting over at age fifteen felt like I was being thrown into the deep end of the pool while never having taken a swimming lesson. I employed that familiar false bravado to cope. My body showed signs of stress: my forehead instantly broke out with quite bad acne for the entire year, which didn't help my confidence. Making new friends seemed daunting, so I concentrated on the familiar: school and golf.

I had earned my way onto the Manitoba Junior Girls team when I was thirteen. Once in Vancouver, with the competition much stiffer, I had to up my game. Also, the season was longer, which only forced me to play and perform more! The upside was that now I was playing with boys—so my interest in golf grew a little stronger. I was getting male attention, but not my dad's. Still, I perceived his love to be in direct proportion to my successes. When I played well, I felt he had all the time in the world for me; when I didn't succeed, I felt emotionally cut off. Our relationship only revolved around golf. He had little to no interest in whatever else might have made me happy.

Sadly, I soon found out that if I underperformed in school and sports, people would like me. When I did better than the other kids, they would mock me and say all sorts of nasty things behind my back. Eventually I learned to cope with the bullying by hiding. I was not taught healthy boundaries. How could my parents teach me about a concept they didn't really understand?

My performance anxiety was well established by now. The competitive label was still hanging around my neck like *a* dog collar, but I really didn't have the cutthroat mindset; I simply took on that role because that's what I thought I had to do in order to be loved. Winning never got me the acceptance I really wanted; it only compounded my false sense of self. I wanted everyone to get along and mostly I wanted everyone to win and everyone to like me. When I beat my competitors, I felt alone.

I learned to play small and never lived up to my potential academically or as a golfer. I sabotaged myself mostly to avoid giving my dad the satisfaction of having a superstar little girl, because I was so angry with him for not letting me dance and follow my other passions like fashion and interior design. I didn't have the vocabulary to express those thoughts or my true feelings; instead, I rebelled at the expense of my personal happiness. By the time I quit competitive junior girls' golf at the age of nineteen, I had absolutely no passion for the game anymore, and my relationship with my dad in particular was strained. I was done. Game over.

Chapter Six—To Burn or Not to Burn My Bra: Is That Really the Question?

My 1976 high school graduation year proved to be very difficult emotionally, for lots of reasons. I managed to make inroads with a few female cliques and even made some friends by that time. I befriended a new girl, Lynelle, whose family had just moved to Deep Cove, close to my school. I totally related to her situation and felt sorry for her. I remember how I felt coming to a new school only a couple of years before, so I went out of my way to talk to her.

Lynelle and her family turned out to be very religious which piqued my spiritual curiosity once again. I envied her and her family life, and I was attracted to how kind and centered and balanced she seemed about … well, everything. Their family graciously invited me to their church and, as encouragement to me to become born again, gave me my first Bible. I would secretly read under my covers at night, just trying to find that something I felt everybody but me already had. I didn't and couldn't tell my parents what I was doing, because by now I was learning to just keep my opinions to myself.

That friendship ended due to the fact that I felt tremendous pressure to convert. I just couldn't—not without feeling like a complete hypocrite. I didn't possess the faith they all talked about. I really,

really wanted to believe, but I still had far too many questions. I had to retreat. The fear of what my small world would think stopped me from exploring further. I buried that empty feeling, and eventually Lynelle and I lost our connection as friends.

Around that time, my mom developed severe sciatica, causing her a lot of pain daily. She suffered from this off and on for many years, but at the start of my last secondary-school year, she was ordered to bed rest for six months as a last resort before surgery. She was not to do any heavy lifting or to stand for long periods. I became her caregiver, the housekeeper, and the cook! Every day I would run home from school to just be with my mom. I felt so bad that she was in so much pain and that she had to stay in bed, and I really wanted to help. I learned a great deal about preparing meals that year, and for the most part I did it willingly. However, looking back now I can see that it probably played a role in the confusion I felt about graduating and moving on. I couldn't see that my mom was ever going to get better, and I felt responsible for looking after her.

I remember on one of my mom's down days, she was starting to confide in me a little. She asked me whether I thought she should divorce my dad. *Wow, you have to ask? Yes* was what I thought, but I didn't really give her an answer. I shouldn't have been privy to this type of information about my parents' relationship, but there it was.

Now I knew that all those years I had felt there was a strained relationship, it had in fact held true … at least for my mom. It would be another ten years before my mom got up the courage to leave my dad, but in the meantime, my thoughts centered selfishly on me. Where would I live? Would I have to choose which parent I wanted to live with? All the normal questions surrounding a divorce overwhelmed me, and my world suddenly started to seem less perfect and very unsafe. The only answer to a perfectionist was to keep on trying harder and to do better. This was one of the first whispers from God that I could only see many years, later. It all centered on trust, men, love, marriage, support and money.

My mom did lose quite a bit of weight while lying in bed that winter. When she was finally able to get up and walk a bit in the spring, she seemed more excited because she'd reached her goal of 128 pounds than the fact that she was up and walking! I remember looking at her new body and saying to myself two things: *I will never get that fat* and *I love her no matter what she weighs*. I was 104 pounds and determined to control my weight. I had tied my entire self-image into being the perfect size five.

On a completely different note and only to compound my uneasiness about everything, my school had allowed me to graduate one month early in late May instead of late June. My golf coach approached my parents with this idea, because I was expected to make the BC and Canadian Junior Girls' golf teams. In order for me to get game ready, I would need to concentrate on golf and put less emphasis on school. They all must have thought I was going to go somewhere with golf, even though I knew, and in fact was pretty determined, that I didn't want to play for a career. Opting out of golf was not an option for me at that time, though—not if I wanted to keep my dad happy. I only had to endure one more summer as a junior golfer, so my secret commitment to golf and myself was to just do it until I turned nineteen.

Succeeding at golf made me stand out. Golf was what I was known for, but it was also what made me feel like I didn't fit in. Concentrating on golf also relieved the pressure I felt to graduate with honors. In my mind, because I wasn't in school for that last month, I could justify not being recognized academically. The school system was letting me off the hook, so to speak. I was playing my cards nicely, or so I thought at the time.

However, golf provided the perfect excuse to avoid the festivities surrounding graduation. I really just wanted one of my male friends to invite me to prom, and then to graduate in an atmosphere of hope for the future, just like everyone else. Back then; if for some reason you didn't get a date to prom, then for sure there must be something wrong with you. I tried to project that I was a winner, despite feeling like a loser. Facing that music would have been humiliating to me; keeping up the façade was once again the only way I knew how to cope.

Then, I met Richard. Coincidentally, one sunny day a few months before graduation, I was taking a bus to my part-time job at a jewelry store in West Vancouver when I caught the eye of a young man. He was twenty to my seventeen (just about to turn eighteen). Our chance meeting that day quickly blossomed into young puppy love for me.

I now felt superior to my classmates. Richard was mature—he had his own place! At least now I felt like I belonged. We were even invited to the cool girl's pre-grad house party. I so desperately wanted to go, but would have felt embarrassed to go without a date.

(Let me just say thank goodness for the progress girls and boys have made in this day and age, when they all go as a group!)

I was not sexually active prior to meeting Richard. I certainly had opportunities, but something inside of me kept me from going all the way. I just never felt ready for that kind of very intimate and personal experience. Nor did I feel that any of the boys I knew were special enough to share that part of me ... until Richard came into my life.

My mom had drilled into me the notion that sex was for marriage only. It was always portrayed as something good girls didn't do. Understandably, I never agreed with my mom's seemingly archaic version of premarital sex; I was a child of the '70s and the '60s, after all. What could my mom possibly know about sex? I was emotionally intelligent enough, or so I thought, to hold out for that someone special. I also knew how to protect myself from becoming pregnant. So I prepared myself, without ever discussing it with my mom.

Well, Richard was that special someone and I very willingly lost my virginity soon after my eighteenth birthday. It was quite magical, as Richard was very gentle, considerate, and patient. I felt so liberated that night, because I was just a stone's throw away from graduating from high school and onto the next exciting phase of my young life.

Unfortunately, two days after my graduation, I received some shocking news from my new love. We found out that Richard was so full of cancer; his doctor was astonished as to how he could still be walking! *Cancer?* I thought Richard was the epitome of youth and health and vibrancy. I remember standing in my kitchen when he reluctantly told me that the reason he hadn't called me for the past few days was because he went to the doctor's office after this rather large lump appeared in the middle of his forehead. He told me he had spent the past few days having multiple tests and it was definitely cancer—a rare form of acute leukemia.

I thought he was joking at first, even though I could plainly see the lump. We embraced and we both cried. I really did not understand the magnitude of his prognosis. I also didn't realize that this tragic news would take me to emotional places that I certainly wasn't prepared for. Now, somehow, I felt even more connected to him than I had before.

The doctors gave him less than a year to live. I grew up very quickly that summer. After I would spend hours on the practice range hitting buckets of golf balls, entering tournaments and playing at least eighteen holes every day, I would rush off to visit Richard in the Vancouver Cancer Clinic or at his parent's home; he had to move back to his parent's house and stop working once he was diagnosed. His chemo, radiation, and bone marrow treatments were aggressive and certainly knocked the wind out of his sails.

I'll never forget the unexpected sound of the telephone piercing our quiet home in the early morning of December 17, 1976, just seven months after we first fell in love. The nurses on the other end of the line said Richard wasn't expected to make it through the night. I quickly threw on some clothes and drove myself to the hospital. The usual fifty-minute drive took me only twenty-five minutes that night. All the lights were in my favor and it was still very early in the morning.

It was just the nurse and I caring for Richard as I watched him take his last breath. He had been in a morphine coma for a couple of days prior to this; by now, his body was shutting down, convulsing every few minutes. The nurse very lovingly told me to sit beside him, stroke his forehead, and talk to him. Meanwhile she held a tongue depressor in his mouth so that he wouldn't choke. She assured me that he could still hear, as apparently, hearing is the last thing to go.

Fragile and fearful myself, I sat, completely mesmerized by the dying process. My heart just opened up. I told him how much I loved him and that it was okay to go. I held him and sadly watched as the space between breaths grew longer and longer until time stood still and there were no more breaths, only empty space. For the first time, I started to wonder: what does happen after death? Do we have a soul, and if so, where does it go? Is he in pain anymore? I wanted answers but didn't know where to get them.

For now, my first love was gone, and more, I felt like I had no one to confide in during my grieving process. I had only ever known my grandmother to die when I was in grade six, and I wasn't even allowed to go to her funeral.

Four days later, just a few days before Christmas, I was spreading Richard's ashes into the Pacific Ocean over the back of a motorboat. There was a small service at his parents' home, after which I never had much contact with his family again. His mother returned the gold chain I had given Richard a few months earlier for his twenty-first birthday. I was grateful for that, for now I had some memory of him and us. I'm sure his family was in shock, but I felt abandoned.

I think my family was equally as stunned by Richard's death as I was, but they were not really able to offer me any sort of comfort. My dad was the only one who ever came with me to visit Richard in the hospital. My mom never visited; she was not comfortable with death. I wasn't either, but I was in love with this man, despite the fact that watching a young, virile man wither away in front of my eyes was quite shocking. Instead, I stuffed down my emotions, as I had learned to do with my family, and I bravely went on.

The truth is that my experience with Richard was simply beautiful in every way. I felt very compassionate toward him and his impending death. We found a connection on so many things that kept us talking and laughing together until the very end of his life.

Life for me went back to a new normal. I did make the Canadian Junior Girls team that summer, but was only an alternate for the British Columbia Junior Girls team. I turned down a golf scholarship in Texas. I was simply out of gas for golf, and for life at that time.

I was so confused by life and death, by love and loss, by marriage and the threat of divorce, by responsibility and freedom—and finally, by realizing that this heartbreaking experience happened to me! My narrow little world had just been blown apart, when previously I had thought I was immune to suffering. I thought I was in control of my life. Bad stuff happened to other people … not to good people like me.

I decided to take a year off from school and work while I got my thoughts in order about what I wanted to do with my life. Richard's sister worked at a credit union, so I applied there and was hired as a filing clerk. After a few months of that, I managed to get promoted to customer service representative. I worked that job six months longer than I intended before I finally enrolled into Capilano College's two-year program in retail fashion design. I was coming out of my funk and finding my stride: not only did I enroll in design school, but I also found a new set of friends. I felt loved and accepted once again.

I realized after completing eighteen months of the two-year program that the retail fashion design diploma was not going to get me as far as I wanted; I had bigger dreams than being a retail manager of a store in a mall. I decided to study marketing, majoring in advertising and sales promotion, at British Columbia Institute of Technology (BCIT)—also a two-year diploma program, but one I reasoned gave me more options for the future.

University didn't really hold much interest for me. At the time an arts degree wasn't worth much … or so I thought. As a very practical person, I wanted something a little more concrete and of *some* interest to me. I really wanted to become an interior designer, but the only interior design schools were in Toronto or Winnipeg, neither a viable option for me. I would have to pay for everything, and I had basically no money. My parents were not in a position to assist me, so I was left to my own devices to further my education, and that meant going to a school where I could live at home.

The interior design manager of the downtown Eaton's store, where I worked in the furniture department, quickly squashed my dreams. For the first time in my life, I reached out to an adult to be a mentor, someone I thought was capable of giving me some sound business advice. He must have had a really bad day that day, because he was quite emphatic when he said, "You don't want to be an interior designer. You work long hours and the pay isn't worth it."

I walked out completely discouraged and crossed that profession off my list. I was so disappointed because in his office, surrounded by nothing but samples of materials and other fascinating decorating items, I had been completely mesmerized. I didn't listen to my gut; I let *his* fear scare me off. *He must know better than I do,* I mused. (Note to self: *never* let anyone put a damper on your dreams.)

I worked three jobs in order to pay for school, books, and eventually my own car. My parents co-signed for me in order for me to get a car loan. I was allowed to stay at home rent-free while I was going to school, but once I graduated and got a job, the free ride was over. While it was tough, I learned to juggle the workload because I so wanted to have my own place, my own car, and an exciting job.

There was no transition time for me; I was a young adult on a mission. The atmosphere at home was strained at best. I was extremely motivated, so with my high energy level, I made it all work. I kept many balls in the air even back then. Successful people and perfectionists don't fail. They just work harder and longer.

This relentless pace would set the standard for what I was about to attract into my life. Little did I know that the stress of it all would show up in many different areas of my life—including my health, which I just took for granted. God was just starting to whisper in my ear. Alas, I wasn't even open to listening.

While it was definitely difficult back then, I look back and think it was the best training ground for me. Those experiences set up some of my strong work ethics that served me well over the years as I entered the corporate world.

My illustrious career in advertising and sales ended as quickly as it began. After graduating from BCIT in 1981, I took the first job offered, but quit after one month. Quitting was not something that I was familiar with, but it proved to be a very wise decision. A straight commissioned sales person I was not. I hated every minute of it. I was disillusioned because I had bought my first pair of open-toed shoes to accent the professional salesperson image I thought I needed to make sales. For thirty days straight in June 1981, it poured. Every night I would go home, dejected and with wet, tired, and very cold feet. This was not what I had in mind for "young advertising sales executive in training."

I was twenty-three by now, and my boyfriend at the time was going to China for a summer exchange program. I felt free of all commitments and responsibilities, except for finding a job in my field. My dad encouraged me to go to Calgary, Alberta, with him for a visit with his brother, so I went. Alberta at the time was booming, and the prospects for my new career were more promising than in BC in the early '80s.

While there I went up to Edmonton for a visit with my older brother Rick and his wife, Laurie. It was the height of the festival season in Edmonton and I was in the mood to party. That's where I met Ted. After a fling-filled weekend with this new man, I headed back to Calgary and applied for some more jobs. After two weeks, I returned to Vancouver with my dad, and shortly after that I was offered a job as a promotion manager at a local shopping mall in Calgary. A mere two weeks later, Ted flew out to help me move. All of my worldly possessions included a black-and-white TV, a stereo, some clothes, and the knife set my parents had given to me for moving out. All I had was hope, as I stuffed my few belongings into my little Honda Civic for my journey to Calgary. But hope was all I needed. My chutzpah and desire would get me the rest of the way; I would prove myself.

I didn't know anybody in Calgary except for my aunt and uncle, who graciously allowed me to room with them for a month. After my month was up, I answered an ad in the local newspaper from a twenty-eight-year-old schoolteacher looking to sublet her very cool condo on the banks of the Bow River. So without any friends once again, I turned to my only comfort: work. I learned a lot in that first year under the tutelage of my first female boss, a woman named Gerry (just like my mom).

Most weekends Ted would drive the three hours from Edmonton to Calgary. Occasionally I would take the bus to see him for the weekend. After nine months of that, Ted proposed marriage. At the same time, my company coincidentally offered a promotion that required a move to Edmonton. I eagerly accepted both offers. Once again, Ted came and helped me move my stuff into what was soon to be our marital home!

With marriage on the horizon, I realized I found myself confused by the working world. At the time, women were agitating for equal treatment; it was the era of burning bras and rejection of the social norms of a previous generation. I didn't think of myself as a women's libber, but I wanted to feel like I fit in with the popular movement of the day. I also couldn't see myself as a stay-at-home in the future. To burn or not to burn my bra ... was that really the question? My role as a female confused me. I knew I earned less than a man would for equal work, and I knew that if I wanted a family, I would be the one to stay home and raise the children. I questioned how I could possibly do it all! But God knows I was going to try.

Something had to give, however, because I never once thought about somebody supporting me in that effort to have it all. I thought I had to do it all by myself. I also thought that having it all only meant having *stuff*. I guess I had buried, at least in my mind, my dilemma over spirituality and religion, because at this point and time in my life, I only desired material success. I was not going to struggle the way I saw my parents struggle.

The thought of being a single mom scared me more than anything; I felt that my kids and I would live a life of poverty. I just never trusted that a man would or could support me either in marriage or divorce. So for me, while I didn't outwardly admit it, I secretly knew that I was destined always to work and look after myself. *I will not depend on a man to support me* became my version of women's lib. Ironically, there was no liberation in that thought.

The advanced notice my mom had given me about possibly divorcing my dad, and then giving myself to my first love and losing him, could all have been influencing factors in my limited thinking back then. I was determined not to let heartbreak and divorces become my reality. I still thought I had control of everything. The glass ceiling was very evident and yet elusive to me, but I promised myself I would keep climbing the ladder to success.

Chapter Seven—Power & Work Addiction: Owning It

In the corporate world, where I strived to be accepted most of my adult life, power was like a drug. Both men and women are attracted to it, and I was no different. I just never realized that women, me included, could wield their own power in constructive ways. I considered myself a reasonably successful businesswoman; however, I never used my power wisely. I played small and silent, mostly when injustices were obvious. It was still a man's world.

I only started to understand my sexual power in my late twenties. I got an ego boost from knowing that I could easily lure men in with my feminine sexuality, even knowing full well that I had no intention of making good on the flirtation. This slow dance of manipulation provided another disconnect for me. If I had only owned my own power, I wouldn't have had to play that game. Back then; I didn't believe in myself enough to know that yet.

The combination of work power and sexual power went both ways. On more than one occasion I experienced some unwanted sexual advances, which I never handled very well. I was engaged to Ted at the time, so I was naively horrified when I was approached in this manner. Once, my boss's boss invited all the staff for an evening of dinner and disco dancing. After a very enjoyable meal and a few dances, he slipped his hotel room key into my palm and said he'd meet me upstairs. On my way out, as I threw the hotel key on the front desk, I stewed about the inappropriateness of my superior's advances. After all, I was twenty-four and he was forty-eight, which made it seem especially gross! I tried to put it out of my mind; I never told Ted, but by the next day, I understood the game. Welcome to the corporate world.

My boss overtly shunned me the next day and gave me a marginal review that week. Even though he hadn't made the advance, I gathered he knew about it, and men tended to stick together. If you refused to *play their games*, then wouldn't advance you. I knew it was unfair: I was an exemplary employee. This would scream workplace sexual harassment today, but in the early '80s, young women who wanted to climb that corporate ladder didn't make waves. I never said a word to anyone.

I quit one month later for two reasons. First, I was getting married at the end of May. After the little incident with the boss, I had asked for three extra days of unpaid time off for my month-long honeymoon. The rest of the time off used my regular three-week vacation. They refused to approve the unpaid time off even though I had put in countless hours of overtime—which I had done willingly, partly to prove myself in my new position and partly because the job demanded it. I mistakenly thought my extra efforts would be recognized and rewarded. They were not.

Secondly, the work place was getting too uncomfortable for me. Rather than pressing charges and creating a scene that wouldn't look good on my resume, I remained silent. But I was really good at that job, so I retaliated by quitting. Their loss, not mine.

After our honeymoon was over, I moved to a new position as tourism manager at the new competitor to my old place of work, the West Edmonton Mall—billed as the largest mall in the world! I stayed with them for only one year, though. I'd thought male domination, intimidation, and sexual harassment was bad at my old job, but this experience made that look like child's play.

The four Ghermezian brothers, the Iranian owners of that mall and well-known innovators in the shopping center industry, had a fascinating rags-to-story, but their ascent in the business world created many casualties. They were not discriminatory over that which they brought down; men, women, competitors, and suppliers all became targets. They were, however, 100 percent loyal to those who were loyal to them. In my relatively naive view of the business world, you just had to be willing to put up with their tactics for a very long time to prove your loyalty and worthiness to them, and you'd make it far.

Big business can be ruthless. The Ghermezians were not afraid to express their feelings at the top of their lungs. One day, I was invited into the boardroom for a meeting with their senior managers. I felt leaving as though my eyes had opened for the first time. This was neither the time nor the place to be timid or to be thin-skinned. For me, it felt like being thrown to the wolves.

As the discussions got more and more heated, the brothers began attacking a female manager for not doing something right, calling her extremely derogatory terms like "slut" and "whore." Much to my amazement, not only did she stand up for herself and deny all accusations, but she started flinging her own insults right back at them. The oldest brother turned on one of the younger men, and then all the brothers began to yell and scream at each other—all in front of their employees! It was like a circus act. All I could see were these wild animals trying to save face by diverting the accusations and attention back onto somebody else. Nobody was willing to accept any responsibility for whatever had gone wrong..

That boardroom incident left me with a lasting worry about whether I wanted to climb this corporate ladder or not. If I did, I couldn't be afraid to defend myself. To survive you had to scream back, or you weren't tough enough to be in that boardroom. I stayed, but my insides were screaming, *Get out!* Maybe I should have retrieved my bra from the ashes!

The straw that broke the camel's back was when I was sent to Toronto to participate in the CNE (Canadian National Exhibition) Trade Fair. The mall was using my *Eighth Wonder of the World* brochure, which I had worked on for months, as the marketing tool to promote this fabulous mall as a world-class tourist attraction.

The Ghermezians wouldn't provide an expense allowance for me in advance, so I had to use my own personal credit card. This might not have been so bad, but they were notorious for not reimbursing people in a timely manner—both employees and many of their suppliers. Ted and I by now had racked up a fair amount of debt funding the start-up of our company, Royal Tours, and I didn't want to risk adding more. I called one of the brothers from my hotel room and insisted he have some money forwarded at least to pay the hotel bill. After an uncomfortable and heated discussion, I walked out of that hotel, with no advance and not having paid for the hotel room. Upon arriving back home, I discovered that one of the graphic designers with whom I had contracted to prepare their promotional brochure had spent three months trying to collect, to no avail. I had had enough; I quit and went to work for my husband and myself.

While I learned a lot in the corporate world, and figuratively speaking, I did grow some balls, it still wasn't enough to prepare me for being 100 percent accountable in my own company, as my own boss. I continued to acquiesce to my husband, now my boss at work. I never felt equal; I felt like his slave. I thought he must know better than I, because he had the master's degree and I didn't. I would soon find out that this wasn't the case at all. I alone finally made the hard decisions to steer the tour bus in the right direction. Eventually, the effects of my addiction to working like a madwoman paid off: I did manage to make the company profitable. When I finally took my first paycheck, I realized my own power ... but it all came at a huge personal cost to my health and me.

Chapter Eight—The Worse Got the Better of Me

I found out I was pregnant for the first time when I was twenty-four, almost exactly nine months to the day before I was to walk down the aisle with my fiancé, Ted. Instead of being jubilated, I was horrified and devastated. I was so ashamed and fearful of what everybody would think, especially Ted's parents, who were strict Catholics. No one in my family knew I was ever pregnant … even to this day, unless they read this book.

I was so disconnected to my feelings and my body back then that I did not stop to question why I was so devastated by getting pregnant even if it was before we got married. I still had so much to prove in my career that being a mother was not even on my list of priorities. To my way of thinking, I had followed all the right rules—using birth control carefully—so why was God punishing me? It had to look a certain way for me: you got married first, and then came the babies. Facing other people's opinions of me, being unwed and pregnant—or worse yet, walking down the aisle in full pregnancy regalia—was more than my frail self-esteem could handle at that moment.

Just at that time, my oldest brother split from his first wife, Laurie, who had become a friend and confidante, after nearly a decade of marriage. Some fifteen years later, Laurie, now remarried to Brian, and I would reconnect and become best friends; in fact, I would call her first to let her know about the plane crash. But at that moment our family supported my brother, so I felt I had no one to turn to who might have understood. And because I had just moved in with Ted, and to a new city, I had no real close friends to confide in once again.

My dad very quickly descended on my brother's situation in rescue mode. In silent anger and shame, I could not face my dad's (assumed) wrath about my pregnancy before I got married. I booked an abortion because I was determined not to have this baby. I even had to stretch the truth to the doctors and counselors who interviewed me to determine my emotional stability. If they knew I was actually going to marry this man, they would never have approved my potential abortion. I would have said anything to get out of it. Coincidentally enough, a week or so before my scheduled appointment, I had a miscarriage. Even though I told the doctor, he insisted that I at least have a D & C (dilation and curettage) to clean things up.

Ted was Roman Catholic, although I was his second wife (he had annulled his first marriage). Getting me pregnant before marriage and then admitting I wanted an abortion was too much for Ted to have to acknowledge to his family. I was so ashamed that I couldn't talk about it, so with characteristic subtlety, I took one day off from work, quietly had the D & C, and then continued as if nothing happened.

Ted and I never discussed it. I never even shed a tear for the potential lost life. I simply swept it under the carpet and never thought about it again until the writing of this book and the unearthing of my past continued.

To compound all this drama, my dad was laid off without any sort of exit package or pension. At the age of fifty-three, with nothing but a high-school education, he found jobs not exactly plentiful. While I didn't witness the day-to-day strain of his new reality, I can only imagine that this was a tough time for him. Looking back, I know it probably represented the beginning of the end for my parents' marriage. Just as I was planning my own wedding, they couldn't help me financially. Not really a problem, just a huge disappointment. I simply scaled everything back, knowing the show must go on!

I was married to Ted at twenty-five. I thought I knew what love was and that I was ready to get married. However, I now replaced my need for my dad's attention with my need to have Ted's attention. I just learned to perform for Ted instead of my father. Only Ted became emotionally unavailable as well. After the honeymoon period is over in any marriage, the real differences start to show up.

Growing up I felt I was loved *conditionally*. I felt that *if* I performed or acted a certain way that pleased others, I received love. This left me feeling insecure as I began relationships as an adult. When I reached out to love my husband, I didn't trust myself to love him fully, nor did I believe that he could love me fully. I never felt anyone was really there to support *if*, and it is a big if, I showed any vulnerability or said my truths. I learned to stifle any and all true feelings, not trusting anyone with them. In return it caused me to only return *conditional* love.

Being naïve, young, and in love, I thought it was my job to support my husband no matter what. I never thought about my needs or wants because as I had learned in my early childhood, I wasn't expecting to get what I wanted and, even worse, I didn't even know I could ask for what I wanted. I still hadn't learned to set boundaries for myself.

Very quickly our new business venture started to not perform up to the projections that Ted had so eloquently laid out on paper some months earlier. All of our savings were gone; our debt had piled up to nearly $150,000; the mortgage on our house was more than the value of it; and the only thing I could think of was to quit my job (the only source of income for us at that moment) and go to work for Ted. In those days, we had some very understanding creditors; otherwise we would have been bankrupt for sure. I thought I could somehow save the day.

And, in fact, it wasn't until I decided to take control and turn the bus around that we actually started to make money. I didn't do it by using my sexual power; I did it by putting my nose down and using my internal smarts to make better business decisions. I dropped the products that were not producing revenue and cut the corresponding costs. Then I started another business in a field for which I really had some passion: I became a meeting planner. Essentially, I functioned as an event planner for the corporate and association world. I planned all their meetings, arranged for speakers, put together charity and fun golf tournaments, arranged for travel, and more. All of my business skills and educational skills dovetailed. The attention to detail in this line of work felt familiar to me. I liked having a lot of balls in the air and felt incredibly accomplished when none of them appeared to fall.

Still, despite my vow of "for better or worse," clearly the "worse" was getting the better of me. I started to resent every aspect of our life even though I willingly let Ted control me, just like I let my father control me with golf. Finally, after several years of toiling sixty-plus hours a week, it became obvious even to Ted that he was going to have to go back to consulting to make ends meet while I would try to make our business work.

I felt like I was always in Ted's whirlwind struggling to keep pace with his relentless pace of work. I thought I had a lot of energy, but Ted could run circles around me. He was a workaholic, as I was too, each with our fears of success as well as failure. We rarely saw each other after he left the business to consult again. We both prided ourselves on not being quitters, so we just kept up the façade that things were fine. We were perfect mirrors for each other.

My second pregnancy came when I was twenty-eight. I was still using birth control, but obviously not successfully. Yet again, I thought the timing couldn't have been worse. By now, both Ted and I were working extremely long hours; I often worked fourteen hours a day or more. Plus, we still didn't have a lot of money. How could we have a baby?

One day, I had put in my typical fourteen-hour day and had not stopped to eat at all. We had nothing at home for food, so we decided to go grocery shopping at ten o'clock that night. I had had severe abdominal pains all day, but was far too busy to pay them much notice.

By the time we got to the grocery store, I was crumpled over in excruciating pain. Ted decided to take me straight to the emergency room. It was a good thing, because less than one hour after being admitted, I was under anesthesia for removal of an ectopic pregnancy. The doctors kept saying, "You are so lucky. It could easily have burst, and you would have died of toxic poisoning."

I had no idea what an ectopic pregnancy was, and I didn't understand that I came close to death. I spent about four days in the hospital before I was released with orders not to do anything—for six weeks! Did they not understand that we were in the middle of our busy summer tour season and I was needed at the office?

True to form, despite the advice from the doctors, I went back to work a good two weeks early and simply toughed it out. I was so disconnected both to what my soul was trying to say and to what my body needed that, now characteristically for me, I just buried any feelings I might have had. For the second time, I didn't talk about it with Ted, or anyone else for that matter. Being pregnant brought shame for me. I was still so not ready to be a mother!

I found out later that having had an ectopic pregnancy meant one of my Fallopian tubes was now removed, and thus a fertilized egg could not go from the ovaries to the uterus. Also, during the operation, they noticed that my other Fallopian tube was severely damaged and resembled a clubfoot. I'm certain that it was due to one of my doctors having inserted a copper IUD into my uterus without removing the old one. I had not yet found a family doctor, so all my visits were to walk-in clinics, where I saw whoever was on duty.

I was advised that the only way for me to get pregnant would be by having in vitro fertilization. In the mid-1980s, the cost of IVF was around $15,000 per shot, and the success rate was less than 5 percent.

For the next few years, both Ted and I went through the motions of being tested to see if we qualified to have IVF done. I don't know why we even bothered; we were so close to bankruptcy that we couldn't possibly pay for the procedure, and we certainly would never have asked our parents. This was not their problem.

I definitely felt I was a failure as a potential mother. I know Ted had desperately wanted to have children, but it didn't look like it was going to happen for us. We checked into adoption, but we found out it could take up to seven years to actually get a baby. By now, I was in my early thirties and unsure I even wanted to consider adopting a child. All I wanted to do was slink under the carpet and make all this heartache go away. Looking back, I can see this was the beginning of the dissolution of my commitment to our marriage.

I started to look outside myself and our marriage for recognition, comfort, love, and validation. Not surprisingly, I found exactly what I needed to fill the emotional gap that existed between Ted and me. I found out very quickly that other men actually found me funny, smart, witty, and beautiful, and it wasn't long before I accepted their advances. Desperate for any sort of positive attention from Ted, I also acted upon my belief that maybe if I looked different he might love me more. This led me to have some elective cosmetic surgeries to correct what I was teased about for most of my life. Not only by my brothers, but also, I must say by some friends. Both something I regret, but at the time, I had convinced myself that this would make Ted love me. It never occurred to me that this might be only their perception. In fact, I really did like my body; I just felt somehow through their constant teasing that there must be something wrong with me and if I could correct this one thing, I won't be teased and I will then be perfect. When I was perfect, I would be loved.

I don't blame Ted at all. I simply didn't know what love really was and what it takes to love not only myself, but also another person. My limiting beliefs centered on trying to change the other person, as I had seen my father try to do to my mother. When it became obvious Ted wasn't going to change, I then turned to changing myself, but from the *outside* only. When that didn't work, I made the decision to withdraw from him and seek what I needed from others.

Still, it took me over four years to get the courage to leave and start again. As we negotiated our way out of our marriage, we finally had a touching heart-to-heart conversation in which Ted promised me he would change his ways. I was too ashamed of all the damage I had done to him and to myself with my unfaithfulness, as well as my inability to provide children for him. I had no mercy, trust, or forgiveness for either one of us left in me. So I left our seven-and-a-half-year marriage to find true love. Maybe the next time it could be different.

Shortly after Ted and I separated, I sat in a park one day and began my fifteen-year search for answers to the age-old questions, "Who am I?" and "What is my purpose?" I was now thirty-two, divorced, and left wondering and wandering. I floundered at best. But I had hope, and maybe even a little faith, that I could be and do better.

I decided to turn to God for the answers, despite not having a lot of experience praying. I didn't know how or if anyone was listening; all I knew was I felt like I was a better person inside than the one who showed up for Ted. I simply pleaded with God, "Show me the way. I feel lost and I don't know what to do!"

Not long after, I attended a self-awareness program entitled, "The Pursuit of Excellence and the Wall." These self-actualization courses gave me the opportunity to create my own personal definition of success. I reasoned this would be a good place to start my new life, so I wrote the following list of what success means to me:

1. To be recognized for my strengths and abilities.
2. To use these abilities to challenge myself and to inspire others.

3. To create beauty and laughter.
4. To be open, honest, loving and intimate in all my relationships.
5. To create peace and harmony in my mind, body and soul.

The important thing for me was not just what the list said, but also what it didn't say. Nowhere on this list did it say anything about material success, travel, or job titles—absolutely nothing to do with external stuff. Instead, it all concerns my inner self, my own unique light. In doing so, I would challenge myself, inspire others, and find happiness. I could be on to something here!

> "Often people attempt to live their lives backwards. They try to have more things or more money, in order to do more of what they want so they will be happier. The way it actually works is the reverse. You must first be who you really are, then you do what you need to do in order to have what want."
> —Margaret Young

Part Two: My Princess Life With Terry

Chapter Nine—Finding Jilly, Like a Leaf Blowing in the Wind

I had been hired in 1989 by the Edmonton Canadian Tire Dealers' Association group to manage their 1990 Annual Convention. This was my first big contract of this sort under Alberta Hospitality, my new meeting planning company. This is how and when I first met and began working with Terry.

It took eighteen months to plan the event, and five days to execute it. I got to know all members of the organizing committee, including Terry and his wife, Carol. I felt they were taking me under their wings and showing me a different side of life while I did my best at creating a successful convention for them. Little did I know then that Canadian Tire was about to become my life, almost from the first day. I am very grateful to them for giving me the opportunity to show them I could do it. It changed my life in a big way.

I'll never forget when I first met Terry. I was waiting outside a room at the Convention Centre, prepared to present my proposal, when Terry came out, shook my hand, and said that they were about fifteen minutes behind. I believe I was the last to present of three possible candidates. He sat with me for about ten minutes and chatted—just making small talk stuff to pass the time. I was a little nervous; I hadn't done anything of this magnitude before, but really wanted to prove that I could do the job. He said, "Don't be nervous! We're all looking forward to your presentation." In those few moments I had with Terry, I did have an intuitive sense that he really wanted me to get the job. Years later, he told me he'd said that because both of the other candidates had failed to impress the group. Fortunately, he liked my style.

Four months after the convention, in January of 1991, I had a lunch meeting with Terry. As the finance chair, I had to present the financial results from the convention to him. As we were chatting, Terry casually asked me what was new in my life. There wasn't much to talk about except the big piece of news, so I blurted out I had left my husband. He did sputter and choke a bit as sipped his wine, but he quickly recovered. No one knew or even suspected I'd been unhappy in my marriage; it would have been unprofessional of me to mix my personal life with my business life. Besides, I hadn't made the final decision to leave until after the convention had ended. I didn't want anything to potentially disrupt my work.

I had no idea then that Terry also wasn't happy in his twenty-plus year marriage, nor did I know he was interested in me. Regardless, I grew to be impressed with him, mostly because of his lifestyle. He was an adventurist in business, which had paid off—he had achieved a lot of success. I respected and admired those qualities in him very much.

Nevertheless, it wouldn't have mattered at that time because I was absolutely determined not to get involved with a married man. I wanted to prove to myself that I could be trusted, that I could be faithful, that I could be a better person than the one who married Ted. I wanted to be the special someone, not the other woman. Ironically, my mother's rather prudish take on sex actually came to be useful for me, as I thought, *why give away the milk when a man will buy the cow?*

I didn't know it at the time, but my philosophy would eventually end up having a positive effect on Terry. Eventually it forced him to make a decision whether or not to take the leap of faith he needed to leave an unhappy marriage—not for another woman, but because it was the right thing to do for him.

Since Terry was married and eleven years older, in my mind, he was not an option for me. Instead, I started seeing another man who turned out to be a disastrous option. I simply wasn't ready. I hadn't taken the time to ask myself, "What do I really want in a relationship with a man?" This was the fuel needed to keep Terry intrigued and very interested in me.

Ironically, my new flame turned out to be married, although he lied straight to my face about that and many more things. I was just far too gullible and naïve to see his deceit. At the time I came to this realization, I did secretly wonder if this was karma playing out: I had lied to Ted, so I was being lied to now.

Terry continued to be in my life as a friend. Over the next year or so, we would meet for lunch occasionally, and he would listen patiently to my woes regarding my divorce proceedings and my new boyfriend. Sometimes I wondered why he was so interested in my life; I was spinning a really good story at the time, but surely he had more important things to do. But he was patient and kind and even somewhat fatherly to me.

Finally, Terry told me that he was very interested in me, but I made it clear that I wasn't interested in him for all the reasons I mentioned above. Still, I could feel that he hadn't given up; instead, he was simply contemplating his next move.

At one point during that time, I wanted to buy a house, but I needed the proceeds from the divorce settlement in order to make a down payment. Generously, Terry offered to loan me the money. We created no written contracts; we just had a verbal agreement that I would pay him prime plus 1 percent.

I was keenly aware that he might have been trying to *buy* me, or at least influence me by lending me this money. Still, he wanted to take the chance on me—even knowing I planned for my boyfriend to live there with me—so I accepted his generous offer.

Even after all that, we almost didn't get together as a couple. Over a Christmas drink, Terry finally confided to me that he and his wife planned to discuss ending their relationship soon after Christmas. He made it very clear that he was interested in having a long-term relationship with me, although first I'd have to get rid of the loser boyfriend. He definitely didn't beat around the bush; he knew what he wanted. You can imagine my skepticism. I was not going to ditch my current boyfriend on the hopes that Terry might leave his wife! I told him, "After you've left her for sure, give me a call." Still, I wasn't really that interested, mostly because I had to see it to believe it. Besides, while my relationship with my new boyfriend was clearly shaky and had been for several months for very good reasons, I found Terry's attitude a little presumptuous. Of course, I could have said no, but I'll admit I was intrigued. One thing tipped the scale in his favor: I knew Terry was honest, honorable, and hard working—all traits that I thought, or rather knew, were inside me.

He and Carol decided it was best for them to split, although they chose to wait until the end of the school year for the sake of their two boys. However, he chose not to mention that part to me. I think he was testing me to see if I would go for his proposal—which I didn't. After three months, I just moved on with my life. I decided to pay Terry back early; my boyfriend had gotten into the deal and decided Terry was a potential threat, so he offered to loan me the money to reimburse Terry.

Fate intervened, though. One day I got a call from Terry. Our conversation was normal and light at first. Then, after fifteen minutes or so of some catching up, he said, "You don't know."

"I don't know what?" I asked.

"You don't know that the check your boyfriend used not only bounced, but he had also *kited* the money. A little stunned at this point, I didn't even know what that meant. So Terry very patiently explained to me what had transpired. (Kiting a cheque is an Illegal scheme that establishes a false line of credit by the exchange of worthless checks between two banks.)

He had known for about a month, but was waiting to see if I would call him. When I didn't, he decided he'd better do some further investigation.

He asked me to lunch again, and that day I was hit between the eyes with some even more startling revelations. He had had my boyfriend investigated by some RCMP friends of his. It seems my new flame had been caught attempting to pick up a prostitute, and that was just one on a long list of other things. No wonder his wife didn't want him either! Terry simply shook his head and said, "You deserve better."

At that moment, I felt like a leaf blowing in the wind, and wherever the wind took me, I would land. I knew in my heart of hearts he was right, but I was embarrassed and ashamed. How could any man do such things—and how could he have done them to me? As I wiped away my tears, I knew that I had to break up with my boyfriend once and for all.

Terry moved in with me the day he moved out of his wife's home. He brought with him a few wildlife paintings, his clothes (all one size too small), his grandmother's rocking chair, a washstand, and a toothbrush. He later told me he didn't want to risk losing me again, so he decided to take the plunge and move in with me immediately. He proposed eighteen months later, at Christmas, six months after that we married at Sooke Harbour House on Vancouver Island. It was a small affair, with just the required two friends as witnesses and a female pastor.

My criteria for marriage were honesty, integrity, and success in business. Terry fit all that and more. I would soon discover that my financial worries could be completely eliminated. When we got together and joined bank accounts, I realized my income paled in comparison to his. The financial pressure to perform just to survive disappeared.

I still chose to work. It was a pride thing, because while many women seek out a man to support them, I believed that men could never be trusted, especially when it came to supporting women. I simply was too stubborn and proud to be a kept woman, which is how I perceived it. Terry really wanted me to do whatever I wanted in the beginning of our relationship, as long as it didn't interfere with his plans. His work and his business became number one.

We did love and respect each other, but the elusive spiritual connection was still missing. I yearned for more—but more of what? I really didn't know. I still struggled with the conundrum of feminist principles. I would love a man to support me, but more emotionally instead of financially. I believed I still had things to prove to myself from a professional point of view. It sounds perhaps as though I was hedging, but it was the truth at the time. Unfortunately, that attitude makes for a difficult starting point from which to grow a lasting relationship. Trust is essential. Around this time, I read *Out on a Limb* and *Going Within* by Shirley MacLaine. My spiritual yearnings were being stirred (if not shaken) because something finally made sense to me. She talked a lot about *chakras* and energy points in the body, and the connection among the mind, the body, and the soul. I would have loved to discuss my interests with Terry, but he just shook his head and either wondered about me or prayed it was just a phase.

I've said I believed there was a higher power I call God, while Terry liked to describe his life philosophy as simply striving to live the teachings of the Ten Commandments. Neither is right nor wrong. I believe Terry found God in nature, not in books or church. I wanted to be special in my husband's life, to be number one. I wanted to be the princess that my family and friends had always jokingly labeled me—a label I was starting to live up to.

The material successes I had spent my life striving for didn't translate to internal happiness. Instead, while Terry constantly worked, I became more and more aware that much was missing from our lives, something that had nothing to do with money or possessions. I was bored with all the trips, the parties, the entertaining, the jewelry, and the beautiful clothes—but I didn't know where else to turn. I longed for that deeply connected feeling not only with myself, but also with my partner. I had all the trappings of a "princess" life; I just didn't feel like one.

Terry had a strong sense of duty, and he showed his love to his family by being an excellent provider. Sadly, his loved ones would have given anything for him to give a little more time with each of us and a little less time at his work, but he was a workaholic ... or, perhaps, a *do*-aholic. I was blinded by this fact when I was falling in love with him because I only saw his success. I once again attracted exactly my mirror; exactly what I still needed to learn.

Unfortunately, Terry didn't think he had a choice and often expressed it to me in that manner. "I don't have a choice," he'd say. "I have to go to work." His ego was working overtime, too! He was externally empowered, and I was number two in his life, second to his work addiction.

I have since learned that the power of addiction (to love, sex, money, work, drugs, alcohol, gambling, shopping, or food, to name but a few) is so strong that one feels powerless over it. Feeling powerless means saying, "I have no choice." All addictions can be overcome, but one must be willing to do the necessary work to do so.

Know this: you *do* have a choice. It's the feeling underneath the addiction—in my case, feeling unworthy, hopeless, unheard, unwanted, and unloved—that you need to deal with. For me, I had to conquer my own addictions of workaholism and perfectionism.

I'm not purporting to be an expert on addictions, but through excavation of all my stuff, I discovered that addictions and limiting beliefs are carried in the cellular memory in our DNA. This is why on a subconscious level we continue to attract the same types of people and situations into our lives—until and unless we are willing to look at these limiting beliefs about ourselves and take the necessary steps to change those beliefs.

While money doesn't make you happy, it does give you choices. After the accident, the choices I made in healing myself included going to alternative healers. Some specialized in BodyTalk (visit www. bodytalksystem.com), a simple and effective form of therapy that allows the body's energy systems to be resynchronized so that they can operate as nature intended. Each system, cell, and atom exists in constant communication with all others. Through the stresses of day-to-day life, these lines of communication become compromised, which then leads to a decline in physical, emotional, and/or mental health. BodyTalk enhances communication, thus enabling the body's mechanisms to function at optimal levels, preventing disease and rapidly accelerating the healing process. I also studied the Belief Change System (BCS), a process using a combination of different modalities of science, ancient wisdom, and inner wisdom to transform self-sabotaging beliefs to self-empowering ones easily and quickly at a cellular level. (Visit www.BeliefChangeSystems.com)

These healers whom I had the good fortune to run across started to help me clearly see the mind-body connection and the emotional baggage that I had held onto for so many years. I finally began connecting all the dots that made up the landscape of my life until then. All I had to do was have the courage to ask for what I wanted and to face the truth.

Chapter Ten—Straight Up the Mountain of Happiness ... One Step at a Time

For the first two years of our marriage, Terry took me on all kinds of adventure trips. While the wilderness was second nature to him, kind of like breathing, to me, it was just plain scary. I always felt like I was outside of my comfort zone. So, like a big girl, I decided I needed to try without him. My first solo mountain adventure took place outside of Whistler, BC, on a nine-day Outward Bound trek in 1997, and I was very proud of myself for completing it.

Terry grew up doing all sorts of outdoor activities and thus always knew exactly what to do, whereas I focused on what color-hiking boots would match my new outfit. Sadly, I'm not kidding. I seriously felt like a fish out of water in the great outdoors. I was, however, always a good sport and I would try almost anything.

The first day of my Outward Bound experience involved going straight up. It was only a one-thousand-foot vertical climb, but it included carrying a fifty-pound backpack—a definite physical challenge for me. I was thirty-seven and had spent my twenties and early thirties mostly in office environments. I didn't have much experience doing anything this physically demanding, but I soon discovered that the only way to scale what seemed to me to be an insurmountable challenge was one step at a time.

Not surprisingly, I was also attached to my grooming routine that included hot showers, hair dryers, make-up, clean clothes, running water, and the most obvious necessity—a toilet! For the adventure, though, we could only bring things from a very strict list of essentials. The organizers weighed our bags when we arrived, and anyone with a bag over fifty pounds had to lighten their load.

Our toilet was a shovel and some instructions as to where to "use" it, so as to not alter the flora, fauna, or nearby streams. I learned to take my shovel and dig a hole to do my daily duties. There was no toilet paper allowed on this eco-friendly trip, so we were taught the type of plant that would be most useful to us. This I paid attention to, for as a kid I remember a few times coming into contact with poison ivy on the golf course. I did not want to confuse poison ivy with an acceptable substitute for toilet paper.

I also found it challenging to cook in the wilderness. We each took turns serving as the cooks for the entire team for a day. I was quick enough to figure out that I would volunteer to make and carry meal one. It didn't matter what it was; at least I didn't have to carry the supplies for the next eight days. I thought that was a pretty good thought for a novice!

During our training, I found learning how to map our location the most difficult. I have a terrible sense of direction. Seriously, to a city girl, all the trees look the same. I muddled through it and pretended like I understood what they taught us, but I never really did. If it were up to me, I would never be put in charge of leading *a* group into the wilderness, but at least I am a willing and good team player.

The second day on the trip, our guides told us that Lady Diana had been killed in an auto accident in France. My long eight hours of climbing straight up were now muddied with the thoughts of how tragic that must have been. Not that I had any thought that my life was anything like her real princess life, but I was starting to realize that some things are out of our control. She had been at the Ritz Carlton in Paris while I slept in a sleeping bag on the side of a mountain. I felt grateful that at least I was alive!

Day four brought rappelling down the side of a mountain. I didn't even know what rappelling was! We all rappelled in the morning; by the afternoon, we were climbing a rather slippery shale slope. Thinking like a team, instead of considering this a competition, still felt new to me, but I was starting to think outside my limiting, selfish box.

I am an Aries, which means I'm a leader with a very strong will. To see that I was only part of a group and that perhaps I didn't have to do it all was a totally new concept to me. I had to learn to trust both myself and other people!

A couple of the members of our team struggled with the slippery shale and with the weight of their fifty-pound packs. I sat there triumphantly, but quickly realized that I had judged these two ladies: they were clearly overweight and out of shape, and I wondered how they ever going to make it.

Then I concluded that we were only as strong as our weakest link. Another lady and I decided that we would hike the thirty minutes or so down the slippery slope and at least carry their packs for them as part of the team effort. Our leaders didn't instruct us to do this; we had to figure it out on our own. The ladies were very emotional and extremely grateful for our assistance. We *all* made it, learning from our own unique circumstances and experiences to grow as warrior women!

The other whisper from God during that trip came when I was awakened from a deep sleep with very strong words repeating incessantly over and over again in my head: "Look after my family! Look after my family!"

That night my foursome chose to pitch our tent a little too close to the edge of the mountain. An experienced hiker would know better, especially given the obvious gusty weather conditions ... but we didn't. We were entirely exposed. I was extremely tired from our fifth day of trekking and my back was feeling the weight of my backpack—or perhaps the weight of my current quandary. Ted, my ex-husband, was involved in a unique hotel project in Waterton Lakes National Park, in Alberta, that would require an interior designer. I was considering taking on this challenge, during which I again would have to rely on my chutzpah to get me through.

Working with Ted was always a challenge. His controlling and perfectionist tendencies always hampered my creativity, but I also knew my own controlling and perfectionist ways got in my way as well. My ego wanted to take on this challenge, but my soul was saying, "No. Look after my family." I needed to go down a *new* path and forget about the past and my lost dream of being an interior designer. I can see now that, even back then, I had a hard time of letting go of the past.

I couldn't sleep due to thinking about those words reverberating in my mind. Shortly after midnight, I crept out of the tent and stared up at the heavens. I just listened to the silence. By now the howling winds had died down completely. The peace in the air echoed the peace I now felt in my mind and body.

The night sky came alive with bright stars and a big, beautiful moon. The lower back pain I'd been experiencing most of the trip had completely disappeared. At last, I knew the answer to my dilemma. I went straight home after the trek, phoned Ted, and said, "No, thank you."

This was huge step for me. I was still trying to play the good girl for everyone, from behind an egocentric mask telling me I could do anything I wanted. I thought I was letting Ted down, but I now had a very distinct knowledge that my new direction was not down that road with Ted again.

(Not surprisingly, when I told him I couldn't take the job, he simply said, "Oh, that's okay!" I wouldn't be surprised to learn he'd never really considered me seriously for the position, and I'd struggled over it for nothing.)

Each of us spent the seventh night on the mountain alone. I felt very uneasy and didn't sleep very well that night. I really had never been alone with myself, certainly not in the wilderness. Of course, that complicates it only if you are afraid … but of the wilderness, or perhaps of yourself?

I failed to use the time for reflection; rather, I simply endured it. While I wanted to be brave and adventurous, I stuck close to my tent, which I had managed to pitch by myself. After all, we had seen a bear a few days earlier; how would I defend myself against a wild animal? For me, however, this was adventure with a capital A to earn my baby warrior status. Would it stick? At least I tried.

Our final day included a ten-kilometer run, the longest I had ever run in my life. My reward for completing it was a tepid shower under a tarp that stretched among a few chosen trees. Stark naked, I showered quickly, shivering as I yearned for the real shower just a few hours in my future, at my brother's house in Deep Cove. Oh, how I lingered in that hot shower! I was exhilarated with my new skills, but very glad to be back to my luxury princess life.

Chapter Eleven—Trekking in India: My Soul's Journey Continues

Three years after my mountain adventure, a girlfriend invited me to join a group of women on a Himalayan trek to India. *India,* I thought. *Sounds exotic and interesting.* I was always looking for a challenge. It was supposed to be a sixteen-day trek into the Himalayas for women over the age of fifty. I would be the exception, as I was only forty-two.

Without much further thought about it, I said yes. Coincidentally, and not surprisingly, everything lined up for me. Linda, whom I knew from Canadian Tire and whom I also credit with telling me that Terry was really interested in me, had agreed to be my climbing partner. I figured, if I could climb to 3,000 feet, what's another 13,500? Shockingly, taking on these kinds of challenges seems normal to me, as my childhood pep talks reverberate in my head. I went from mere foothills in Canada, comparatively speaking, to the highest peaks in the world, with little trepidation. I thought it might be a physical challenge, of course; I had no idea the trip would serve as a catalyst on my one step at a time journey to my soul's purpose. My spiritual senses were going to be teased and awakened even more.

In preparation for our trip, the organizers highly recommended that we each partake in some form of exercise program for six months. True to form, I started fourteen months early. I diligently hired a trainer who helped me pack on the muscles. I realized later that I added a good twenty pounds too much. I was pretty bulky and not feeling exactly comfortable with my new sturdy, stocky body. But at least I was strong enough to lug my pack up those mountains!

In a bit of a digression, I should note that at this juncture in my life I decided to send what I thought was a love letter to my dad. I dropped the letter in the mailbox the day before I left for India, in the hopes that upon my return I would have a much closer connection to my dad. By now our normally strained relationship was bursting at the seams ... at least for me.

A couple of incidents with my father had completely embarrassed me in front of Terry, which got my blood boiling. As was our usual manner of communicating, we both shut down and these occasions were never discussed. So I thought, in an effort not to burn bridges, I would outline for my father all the things that I had learned and appreciated about him; and then I would ask what he would be prepared to do to have an honest relationship with me.

The effort backfired. My dad was extremely hurt which resulted in the emotional game I was familiar with: he cut me off. Despite efforts on the parts of my brother Steve and other family members to get us to reconcile, my father still refused to talk to me. He even hung up on me when I called at Christmas time.

This charade continued for nearly two years, until one day I called him and strongly suggested we practice some active listening with each other. At the end of that telephone conversation, I asked that we finally drop all the hurt feelings and never talk about it again: the past is the past and all will be forgiven.

Throughout my married life, Dad harshly judged my husbands. When he was done with them, he would turn his judgment back on me in the form of making unnecessary comments about my weight.

Somehow, neither my husbands nor I were ever good enough for him. But after that conversation, my dad was like a puppy dog with me. In his way he was trying. However, I was never able to get over my own deep hurt and resentments. He never lived up to my lofty expectations; at that time, I was the one who couldn't forgive.

Meanwhile, I headed off to India. We landed in Delhi shortly after midnight on September 6, 2000, and were immediately met with a surprise. We found out that our group now included a sixty-one-year-old man named Mike, from New Zealand. Despite his rather "stiff upper lip" British-style persona, he proved to be a welcome part of our (previously all female) trekking team. In fact, Terry and I had a wonderful visit with Mike and his wife in Taupo, New Zealand, five years later.

At that time, I was still running Alberta Hospitality, my meeting planning business. After about seven years in the field, I'd decided to get some credentials behind my name. I got certified as a CMP (Certified Meeting Professional) in 1995. In my usual manner, once I validated my own talent, my interest waned. This continued a pattern with me: about four years into my marriage with Terry, I was again looking outside myself to find something that would challenge me and keep me searching for that elusive purpose in life. It wasn't until I climbed a few very high peaks in India that I admitted to myself I still truly wanted to be an interior designer. I couldn't quite fathom how becoming an interior designer would happen without turning over the apple cart. I had the interest, the desire, and yes, some talent; I just had no formal training and believed Terry wouldn't support me in this endeavor. Instead, I chose to find my life's meaning (or so I thought at the time) in the Himalayas. For now, the high peaks were calling. Still, it was there that I decided that I had to go for my dream and not wait any longer. I just didn't know the *how* or the *when* for fulfilling my life-long dream.

Our trek included fifteen nights of sleeping on the ground and climbing to altitudes of 16,500 feet, all of which proved to be extremely challenging. Acclimating to the lack of oxygen and the resulting maladies—severe headaches, confusion, nausea, and sleeplessness—took some getting used to. Even though I only had to carry a ten-pound backpack with just the essentials (a sweater, camera, water, and rain gear), I still found it more difficult than carrying the fifty-pound pack back in BC.

Before, I had figured that this would be like luxury trekking! A team of Sherpa's and their horses carried our food and all of our camping gear. All of our meals were prepared for us; our tents were put up for us when we arrived at camp after the usual six or eight hours of trekking. I soon found out that because of the difficulty of the climb, all I could muster at the end of the day was to *fall* into my tent. My appetite was minimal due to altitude sickness, despite our exhausting days. After our afternoon chai tea that was delivered outside our tent, we would prepare for an early supper around 6:30 P.M., and then it was bedtime. There is no electricity that far up, so our only source of light was our headlight (a flashlight strapped to our heads) and the stars.

Despite the exhausting, yet exhilarating, days, the lack of oxygen at such high altitudes made it difficult to sleep. After the first eight days I also realized that I was allergic to Linda's down sleeping bag. I had forgotten to tell her I was allergic to down. Once I switched tent partners, my sleep improved.

Our trek started at the very end of the monsoon season in India, thus leaving the mountain slopes quite slippery. A few hours into our climb on day one, a horse lost its footing and fell over a slippery slope down a ravine a good one hundred yards down. Thankfully the horse was not hurt, but my sleeping air bag was; the nozzle broke in the fall. The only thing that was supposed to cushion me on the hard ground for the next fifteen nights had broken. Now *this* was roughing it, especially for someone like me.

As I acclimated, my desire to connect —my spirituality, if you will—started to really ache in me. Maybe by osmosis, something from these seemingly happy, peaceful people seeped into my blood. I wanted what they had. It reminds me of the funny line in the movie, *When Harry Met Sally* …. Meg Ryan's character fakes an orgasm to her friend, and the woman at the next table exclaims to her waitress, "I'll have what she's having!"

India is a country of contrasts. Its natural magnificence overshadows the extreme poverty that you see almost everywhere you go. It harbors a surprising peacefulness, a chaotic orderliness, and a humble happiness that I was just starting to comprehend. Spirituality oozes from every pore from every person in India. How could they possibly be so happy when they had so little?

Our first hotel was a complete culture shock. The brochures proclaim it as a four-star hotel. It was, nothing like any four-star hotel I've ever stayed in. Okay, it did have air conditioning, two separate single beds and a bathroom with a bucket shower. You filled the bucket with water and created your own shower! I shared the room with Linda, my hiking partner, who would become my life-long friend. Little did we know that after we left Manali, we wouldn't even have a bucket shower for another sixteen days. This was all part of India that really had to be taken in stride.

The beauty of this trip was that we were *with* the people. There was nothing luxurious about this trip at all, and because of that, it was so much richer an experience than if we had just visited the tourist attractions and stayed in the five-star hotels that pepper Delhi's streets. I learned later that most of the southern part of India is teeming with riches—a complete contrast to the poverty everywhere in the northern mountainous region. In fact, it makes the richest citizens of North America look, to use India's own terms, lower caste.

Riches as I knew them were not visible to my naked eye, but still utterly permeated the air; the kind of riches that I would yearn for later, spiritual connections to God. In India they had hundreds of gods, and while I don't completely understand the religious teachings of Buddhism or Hinduism, I was open to learning. I could feel their inner joy! I wanted that. I'll take even just one deity if it means I can capture their joyful essence that was just so obvious.

We also saw an array of animals, including the sacred cows, dogs, monkeys, elephants ... you name it. We even saw snake charmers. All of this animal life peacefully co-mingled with a myriad of people, cars, trucks, and motorbikes. Basically there are no rules, as there is an understanding of co-existence. A short honk of the horn alerts the car in front of you that you want to pass them ... so you do. Then very shortly they pass you with a polite honk in return. There was no road rage; everyone understood the organized chaos and politely went on with their business. We were often within inches of a very fast moving vehicle of some sort that respectfully weaved its way through the narrow streets and unpaved highways. I was exhilarated and felt incomprehensibly safe.

Luckily our group leader was an extremely efficient guide named Robin Ross. She had come to India from New Zealand ten years earlier during her own self-proclaimed midlife crisis. She fell in love with the country, as well as with a Hindu guide named Yoga. Together, they formed a company taking Westerners on adventure holidays all over India.

Robin had a home in Manali, north of Delhi, next to Yoga's home, which he shared with his wife, Dugli, and their two children. Even though Robin and Yoga were lovers, everybody was happy with the arrangement. Dugli viewed Robin as having brought riches to their family—Yoga was now employed for most of the year, which kept her family from suffering in poverty, as so many other families in their close communities did. While this type of arrangement is taboo in our society, I chuckle to myself; after all, how many women really wouldn't mind this arrangement? Who was I to judge what worked for them? One evening Dugli even made us supper and dressed us in traditional Indian garb. Everyone laughed, smiled, and enjoyed each other's company.

The smell was shocking at first. After only a few days in Delhi, I began to notice that it was difficult to breathe, as the pollution from the millions of vehicles began to stagnate in my lungs.

We spent the first few days just drinking in the culture, so fascinating and just so different from anything I had ever experienced for myself. Poverty existed everywhere you looked, and yet vibrancy buzzed in the air. People washed themselves, their dishes, and their clothing in the streets; ate their food openly with their fingers (right hand only); squatted anywhere and everywhere to relieve themselves; and simply carried on with their daily lives as best they could. I found the begging bothersome at first; we were explicitly advised not to give money to the children, but I felt guilty. Robin believed that this only contributed to their dependency to beg. Regardless, sometimes we would succumb and give them something, as many were clearly poor and starving.

It was in India that I also felt what it was like to be a second-class citizen. We stuck out like sore thumbs among a sea of dark skin. Here, *they* stared at *us*. I found this state of being , like the saying the shoe is on the other foot, very hard to take and was secretly glad when we were whisked away to the northern region of India, away from so much poverty.

We boarded a train for our 245 kilometer trip north to the city of Chandigarh for a next-day excursion to the Kullu Valley and the city of Manali. After three days of acclimatizing to the twelve-thousand-foot altitude and the lack of oxygen, we finally met the team of horsemen who would very skillfully guide us through treacherous mountain passes, over rushing rivers, and up very steep climbs for the next sixteen days. They wore fifty-cent rubber flip-flops—and we wore four-hundred-dollar sturdy leather hiking boots. What a contrast!

We soaked up the culture by stopping every so often to visit one of the many temples. One day we caught a ceremony at a Hindu temple. Leaving our shoes at the door, we humbly entered the cave-like structure built into the side of a rock wall and sat in silence.

The cave was lit only with candles, and there were many pictures and statues of the Hindu gods. We listened and watched with reverence. We had no idea what the worshippers were saying or to whom they prayed, but it didn't matter; we could feel their reverence for their gods.

The train ride out of Delhi was a complete eye opener. For hundreds of miles, I observed nothing but primitive shantytowns and scattered garbage. It was shocking how widespread the poverty was. People were everywhere; we would have to wait until we were 16,000 feet up the mountain before we felt the solitude that we all were seeking. As far as the eye could see on a very flat horizon there were people—occasionally without a stitch of clothing. Then you'd catch a glimpse of an Indian woman dressed in a beautiful bright sari, illuminating her happy face. Everyone greeted us with the traditional folding of the hands in front of the heart, a bow of the head, and then the familiar, "Namaste." They were all so humble. We learned that the people of India wasted nothing: even the cow dung is dried and used to build a house or hut.

Finally we began our climb. The highway up to the top of the mountain included men herding their sheep and the occasional guru. There were no paths, and certainly no roads; instinct guided the experienced shepherds up and around these mountains like it was nothing. They offered *chai* tea (black tea with a lot of milk and sugar) to anybody passing by, and they considered it an insult to them if a passerby didn't stop and have tea.

A couple of very funny things happened. About day ten of our sixteen-day trek, I got my period. By now we were all familiar with the bathroom routine. Kindly and respectfully, the team of horsemen would erect a red tent-like structure somewhere close to our camp to dig our hole, do our business and cover it up. On one very rainy day, we arrived early at our camp for the night. I had a few hours to actually relax and dry off. Reluctantly I got up from the comforts of my dry tent, put on my rain jacket and boots, and headed toward the red tent. All of a sudden, a huge gust of wind came up and knocked the poles out of the ground. I was left hovering over this hole with the tent now stuck to my bare behind, trying to change my tampon and still trying not to make any fuss. However, the blowing tent and my noises alerted the Sherpa's, who quickly came to assist me. Embarrassed, but grateful, I managed to cover myself and not fall into the hole. We all had a really good laugh at the absurdity.

They fashioned a wooden pole to hold up the tent. I have no idea where they carried it from; it's not like there was a forest nearby. They probably had to search for hours for the right tree to cut down to pole size. They were amazingly handy at finding the right stuff to always make things work.

A few days later, that wooden pole would come in very handy. We were climbing our last ascent up a glacier. All of a sudden, I heard a commotion and looked up to see two horses sliding down the glacier toward us! Gupta, one of the guides, was poking me with the pole and firmly suggesting that I get out of the way of the horses. I was having difficulty breathing and moving, so all I could do was move as though I were in a movie and the action had gone into very slow motion. I exclaimed, "I know, I know, I'm moving as fast as I can!" In fact, our movements were exaggeratedly slow, and I was *just* able to step aside and watch as the horses and horsemen slid past Linda and me.

Once on top of our final mountain pass, we stopped and celebrated another victory. We offered thanks to the many gods, prayed for our survival, and after a few pictures and a brief rest went back down the slope. Camp for the night was still a good four hours away, but at least it was downhill.

Near the end of our trek, we came upon a small village where we camped out in the fields, literally among the cows and oxen. That particular night, a huge thunderstorm rolled through the area. We awoke in our tents to some very loud and insistent mooing. It turns out they sensed the storm well before it actually happened.

The heavens opened and loosed torrential downpour—and I mean torrential, such that we thought for sure our tent was going to float away! The thunder and lightning now lit up our yellow tent like electric lights. At close to 14,000 feet, the storm was utterly unlike anything I was used to in Canada, where there is often a ten-second delay between the lightning and the sound of thunder; here, the two occurred simultaneously. It was Mother Nature's symphony: the cows, the oxen, and us inexperienced Westerners. I was entranced, mesmerized by the voracity with which Mother Nature cleansed her earth. I opened up the flap to the tent and simply sat in awe. The other ladies were not as enthralled, but to me it was like front row tickets to the best concert I could think of. I loved it!

The end of our trek loomed, which seemed to infuse me with energy; I literally skipped over the large slate boulders as we headed downward, and I could finally breathe more easily. My first thoughts turned to having a shower and putting on clean clothes. It had been at least sixteen days since I last looked in the mirror ... but somehow, I didn't really care.

After we came down the mountain, we had a few more days in McLeod Ganj, the home to the Dalai Lama. Robin had requested an opportunity for our group to meet with him, but unfortunately, he was out of town. He returned just as we were leaving; we witnessed the streets lined with hundreds of people all waiting for a glimpse of his Holiness to arrive back by limousine.

Our time in MacLeod Ganj was not wasted, however, as we got to visit many other Hindu temples. One morning Linda and I got up at six o'clock to experience the morning chanting of the monks.

Unfortunately, something else was happening in the town square that particular morning, but by late afternoon we finally got to enjoy the deep, mesmerizing sounds.

We visited the Norbulinka Institute of Art, where exiled Tibetans uphold their culture by expressing it through art. There I met our next tour guide. We had an instant connection, but we couldn't figure out why until we discovered that he and I had been at the same tourism conference in Bali twelve years earlier. In fact, I had celebrated my thirtieth birthday there! I had come halfway around the world and coincidentally met a person who seemed familiar—and was now talking about reincarnation. It awakened something in me. Was it coincidental and synchronistic? Both, I'm sure.

We spent the afternoon listening to his personal beliefs about reincarnation. At that moment, I did have this intuitive feeling that I had had a life either in India or perhaps with this tour guide. It was an afternoon I will never forget.

Our next adventure was to the city of Agar, the home of the Taj Mahal, one of the Seven Wonders of the World. Our schedule took us to see this incredible monument on the same day that Indians (Westerners call them East Indians, but they call themselves Indians) celebrated their national holiday for the death of Mahatma Gandhi. Tens of thousands of people all wanted a glimpse inside this spectacular architectural monument, built by a prince for the love of his life.

While we all waited in line on an extremely hot and muggy day, I regrettably had the urge to use a bathroom. I excused myself from the line and asked my friends to keep my place. The closest bathroom was about half a mile away. I grabbed a few coins for the attendants, slipped away, and ran all the way to the bathroom. I didn't want to miss getting inside the Taj! Alas: by the time I got back to the line, my friends were just coming out; I ran into them as they were trying to find their shoes. The marble, heated by the searing sun, made it impossible for us to stand in bare feet, so everyone kept hopping vigorously from foot to foot.

My friends motioned wildly at me, not to go inside. They were pointing to the armed police at the single door who were aggressively shoving mobs of people around. My friends were quite insistent that I not go inside and assured me it was nothing great, basically a lot of inlaid semi-precious stones and a few crypts. They obviously knew something that I didn't. I quickly realized this wasn't the time to protest. That was it. All this way ... for what? But I had safety on my mind now, as I could sense that something could get out of hand rather quickly and I didn't want to be caught in the middle of it so we immediately left.

Our trip would end soon; I was anxious to get home to see Terry. Communication was limited at best while I was in India. We did manage a few e-mails, although the Internet in cafes in India in 2000 was really slow. Sometimes in the evening we would spend hours trying to connect, and then it wouldn't be for perhaps a few more days or even a week before we were someplace that we could check to see if we had received a reply. It seemed kind of fun this way. I can only imagine what it would have been like to have your loved one in a war overseas and wait for a letter by post!

Once I got back to Canada, I can honestly say that it took me a good six months before I started to be a true consumer again. The trip had changed me significantly: I felt more gratitude for what I did have in my life, but I also knew that there was still something missing—and that material possessions would not make me happy. I was still searching for that connection to something. So my searching continued, one step at a time ... and this time I started to think about looking inside for happiness.

Chapter Twelve—Nudges from God:
The Owl in the Burnt Out Tree

One October morning in 2001, Terry had to attend an early Rotary breakfast, so—rather uncharacteristically—he asked me if I would walk Duffy, our Springer Spaniel. Looking back, I can say this was one of several nudges from God that I had already received, but it was the first one I was willing to actually listen to.

The night before, I had attended my first class on *chakras*, the seven energy points in your body. During the class it became clear that I had some blocked energy in the third chakra, around my solar plexus. I knew instantly that this was God's way of sending me a message through how my body was feeling that I needed to assert my will on a decision that had been plaguing me for quite some time: I wasn't following my passion. In fact, I wasn't even close to admitting that I might have a passion other than being Mrs. Terry Douglas. Being someone's wife did not meet my needs in terms of recognition; playing small didn't satisfy me anymore.

That particular morning was a little foggy. As I was walking Duffy in the woods behind our house, I came to a fork in the path. One way led toward our house, one away from it. Suddenly Duffy stopped in his tracks and stared up at a burned-out tree that stuck out like a sore thumb in the middle of the woods. I stopped beside him, and together we looked up to see the most incredible owl perched on the topmost branch. The moment felt surreal; the owl appeared unusually large and even somewhat illuminated, its neck and head rotating from side to side as if it were looking at the fork in the road. In its wisdom, the owl seemed to tell me, "You're on the right path; just take it."

In that brief moment, I looked down to shake my head, not believing my eyes; when I looked up again, the owl had completely disappeared. I'd heard no sound, not even a flutter of wings. I looked at Duffy and he looked at me. Invigorating energy infused my body; I skipped the rest of the way home. I knew without a shadow of a doubt that the blockage in my third chakra existed to tell me to talk to Terry about something. I just hadn't had the willpower to do so.

Always a skeptic back then, I still needed more evidence to reassure me. The next day I walked Duffy again and said, "Okay, God; if you sent a wise old owl to deliver a message, or to nudge me along, show me another owl within seven days!" All that week, I stewed about telling Terry that I really wanted to go back to design school, preferably in Calgary. While Terry supported me, he wasn't keen on interrupting our life just so that I could follow my dream. "Why aren't you happy supporting me and taking care of the dogs and our busy life?" he would ask. Sheepishly, I wouldn't answer because I never felt worthy enough to ask for what I really wanted.

Still, a mere year earlier I had had the epiphany in India about finding my passion in life. I didn't want to regret not doing something in my life that I was passionate about before I died or before Terry retired. I felt trapped, thinking that once Terry retired, my hopes and dreams would all be over because I'd have to retire too!

I imagined that my passion wasn't exactly going to fit with Terry's idea of what I was supposed to be doing. I didn't want to rock the boat in any way that would disrupt Terry's smooth sailing through life, which meant I looked after him, tended to the dogs, and made myself available to help with his business. That was our unspoken agreement: I support you, you support me. We made that work on a day-to-day basis. Secretly, of course, it wasn't working for me—in fact, it was eating me up. I was often blocked and had many physical pains in my body … I just wasn't ready to connect all the dots. So I stewed instead. This silent anger showed up in my digestive system as well as back issues. I was constipated a lot, despite my workouts and healthy eating. I simply held onto my emotions rather than express them.

Finally, I mustered all the courage I could and told Terry on Saturday night. I was quite calm and collected by this point, because I knew I was sharing an important truth. I started with the owl story, at which he scoffed and called it a mere coincidence; there must be lots of owls in the woods. I knew differently; I had walked there many a day and never seen one. At the end of my story, he didn't exactly rejoice and encourage me, but he didn't say no. He simply implied that going back to school was fine as long as it didn't interfere with our lives.

The next morning I woke up, opened the front page of the *Edmonton Journal*'s Life section, and beheld a half-page picture of an owl. Did I need any more nudging? Nope! It was up to me now. At the same time, I couldn't let any balls drop.

I found a way to get my needs met, but on a much smaller scale than what I really wanted. I enrolled in a course in residential interior design at the University of Alberta, located in Edmonton. It took me four years of night school and some very tricky social planning on my part to make it all work, but I did it—and, I might add, I graduated with distinction, because of course I was still an over achiever!

In addition to going to school, I went to work in a very small home decor store that provided outside design services. I quickly grew tired of working for someone else, though, so I branched out and started my own business. I really enjoyed my career as an interior designer; I thought I was in heaven. I still managed to keep the balls in the air with respect to managing our social life, and I kept up with my exhilarating career in design. I was happy ... or so I thought.

> The Owl is the silent guide, teaching us to trust our instincts and silent impressions, especially in regards to spirit communication. Its appearance now is alerting you to much spirit activity around you. The owl is also a creature of the night, and night symbolizes the darkness within – the places where great secrets and great treasures are hidden. Spirit is around now to remind you of this and to help you uncover those treasures. The owl provides guidance through heightening your senses – physically and spiritually. Its eyes are adapted to see the subtlest of movement with the least amount of light. Because of this, you will see subtleties that you may not have noticed before. Its hearing is just as acute as its sight. Owl is telling you that help and guidance are available to you, but it is still up to you to act upon it.
>
> —Andrews, Ted, *Feathered Omens; Messenger Birds from the Spirit World,* Jackson, TN; Dragonhawk Publishing, 2009.

Chapter Thirteen—The Lure of Storm Watching

Our lives continued to be busy and full. My design business flourished, as did Terry's Canadian Tire store. Every year for perhaps the past five years, Terry's financial results exceeded even his own expectations. Despite this, Terry continued to raise the bar. His financial goals kept expanding; whatever it was, it was just never going to be enough.

I needed a break that included some quality alone time with my husband. All I had to do was convince him to go along with it and we would be off on a mini-vacation. The year before, in January 2005, Terry and I had taken our first ever three-week vacation together to New Zealand … alone. Our vacations had always included at least one other couple. My expectation was that we'd do something similar or at least as grand again this year, so I was a little miffed when Terry told me in October that he was planning on going on a one-week vacation the following February with his hunting pals. I was not invited.

Terry regularly took one-week vacations—that wasn't why I was annoyed. However, this news accompanied the announcement that, since his store was going through a renovation in August, we wouldn't be going on our winter vacation that year. That left me stuck in St. Albert in the middle of winter.

After I expressed my disappointment, Terry agreed we could have a quickie vacation, and he encouraged me to book a trip wherever I wanted to go. I appreciated that he was willing to at least do that.

I checked out a one-week vacation somewhere warm, perhaps in the Caribbean, but after considering the two days of travel that it required getting there and two days back, I concluded it wasn't worth it. So I made the decision to go somewhere closer and less expensive. My intention behind this was simply to spend some quality time with Terry to hopefully reconnect before he headed into his busy season and his store renovation.

Finally, I booked a four-day, five-night "Storm Watchers" package at the famous Wickaninnish Inn, a luxury spa resort, in Tofino. I planned it for January of 2006, when the break from the wintry weather would be most welcome—and furthermore, selfishly, I was excited to get away with my husband for a few days.

The "storm" element truly appealed to me. As a little girl, I loved to sit with my family on the front steps of our Winnipeg home and watch the storms roll in just before bedtime. Cuddling with my dad, safe and comforted, is when I felt the most loved. This one childhood favorite memory led to a series of synchronistic events that changed my life completely.

Finally, January came. We arrived in Tofino, a small coastal town on the west side of Vancouver Island, via a commuter plane from Vancouver. The plane itself was not nearly as nice as it is pictured on the website, but I had no intuition that this would be our final five days together. It wasn't until much later that I learned that the pilots joked among themselves that the website showed a much nicer plane than the one they actually flew. In fact, the maintenance of the planes was questionable and had been under scrutiny by Transport Canada for quite some time.

I chose the airline, Sonic Blue, based on the flight times I found online; the pictures and prices were all comparable to the competition. If I had chosen a different airline, we would have gone out on Wednesday instead of Tuesday and thus missed a whole day of togetherness. I simply made the wrong choice in that moment. Or did I?

The odd thing, though, was that as soon as I told Terry about the travel arrangements, he questioned me quite a bit about this new airline. I was a little taken aback by what I thought were unreasonable questions. At the time I thought he didn't trust that I could have done this all online, all by myself. I now wonder if, in fact, he simply was having a premonition of what was to come.

Around the same time, he started to suggest that he intended to write his own obituary. *Who thinks of things like that?* I wondered. I just thought that was a bit controlling and he was being a bit presumptuous ... like somehow we wouldn't do one for him someday!

Still, I grew excited about the trip. A few years prior, Terry had surprised me at Christmas time, with the same package. I thought it was one of the most thoughtful gifts he had ever given me, besides the box filled with tools to help me in my design business. Those two gifts outshone all my diamonds or other expensive jewelry he had ever given me.

In February 2004, we spent a magical week at the Wickaninnish, but unfortunately there were no storms. In fact, the whole week was unseasonably warm and calm. Maybe this time, we'd actually see some winter storms. Additionally, I added the highlight of a couple's massage in their famous cedar hut perched over the Pacific Ocean. It sounded so romantic, a must-do for me. I was very particular orchestrating the arrangements with the spa coordinator. If there were no storm, at least then we'd have this romantic plan!

We arrived on Tuesday, so I wanted the massage on Thursday afternoon, just before our pre-dinner ritual of sharing a half bottle of champagne and a bag of microwaved popcorn. The perfect place to storm watch was from the two comfortable chairs conveniently placed in front of the huge picture windows of our large private suite. With the fireplace blazing in the background, I was finally able to be alone with Terry and share some quiet moments in which we talked, we laughed, and we shared. This always made me happy!

Thursday afternoon arrived; I was full of anticipation. I really wanted Terry to enjoy the massage, too. To my disappointment, when we checked in a half hour early to enjoy the steam sauna, I was told that we would be in the main lodge. I was positive I had booked the cedar hut. I silently fussed all that night, not knowing if I should say anything.

While I was having my manicure the next morning, I found my voice and I mentioned my disappointment and surprise to the spa attendant. She checked, and then apologized to me when she discovered the mistake. Immediately, she asked how she could make it up to us. At this point, Terry didn't even know the difference, but for me, the cedar hut experience remained the primary reason for going to Tofino and not the Caribbean. I just wanted to know what had happened.

She suggested a full refund of our money, which I graciously refused; instead, I hoped we could still have the experience I'd planned. As fate would have it, the only time they had available in the cedar hut was at 9:00 A.M. on Saturday, January 21. Since our plane wasn't leaving until 1:30, I thought that would be perfect.

On Friday, our final full day together, we put on our galoshes and rain jackets and headed into town to explore the art shops. Shopping for art together was a favorite pastime of ours. However, that day we only purchased a workout top for me and a pair of socks for Terry. Did I mention he had an obsession with socks? I gathered that as a child socks were hard to come by for him.

After we finished our shopping, we decided to take a bit of a detour to check out some real estate in the area. It was there that we talked about our future plans. We decided against purchasing a vacation property, hoping instead to play more golf—still a passion for both of us. After our detour, we once again walked the famous mile or two of beach that attaches to the Wickaninnish. Just as we were coming to the last hundred yards, Terry stopped, pulled our digital camera from his pocket, shoved it in my hands, and said, "Take a picture of me." Surprised, but always willing to cooperate, I did. He posed on a rock where the ocean and the shore filled the background.

Then he said he would take a picture of me. Again I obliged. At the time, I thought it was a rather odd thing for him to do.

As we walked back to our hotel room, we bumped into a young couple from Victoria whom we knew quite well. In fact, he was the son of the couple who stood up for Terry and me when we married. I said to Terry, "Isn't that Laura and Mackenzie Kyle?" After some brief hugs, we asked them if they would join us for dinner. We parted ways, each of us pleasantly surprised by our chance meeting.

This last supper, so to speak, was very pleasant. Mackenzie was a very forward-thinking young entrepreneur; Laura, a very proud mother of two small children. While talented in her own right and clearly a very strong support to Mackenzie, she was happy at this point in her life being a mom. I always admired her, as she seemed to have no issues with giving up her work life for motherhood. Because of my issues with being controlled by a man or his money, I always maintained some autonomy in terms of continuing to work, even though Terry tried to convince me to not work at all. I always admired women who trusted enough to be stay-at-home moms—and was happy to boot. I could never quite figure that out.

I recall Terry being quite animated that evening, as I know he truly felt proud to have mentored Mackenzie as a young boy. It was fun listening to a younger generation talk about their dreams, as we had spent the week very much talking about ours. The evening ended very pleasantly as we parted ways around ten o'clock.

The next morning, I awoke early. I truly love Tofino, with its towering trees and ocean breezes. Did I have a premonition of what was to come later that day? I don't think so, but I'm not so sure Terry didn't.

Our massage in the cedar hut proved to be everything and more than I had imagined. Even Terry agreed that the view took his breath away. I felt complete; even Terry felt relaxed. The rest of the morning was somewhat uneventful, as we prepared for the shuttle to take us to the airport at approximately 12:30 P.M. We enjoyed one last scrumptious brunch together in the main dining room overlooking the Pacific Ocean.

As we waited patiently in the hotel lobby, I took a few more pictures of the inside of the hotel, thinking that someday I would like to replicate some of the spectacular West Coast design ideas in the house that we were going to retire to in Kelowna. The decision about where we would live in our retirement was already made; we just weren't sure of the when. In 2002, we thought it would be 2008 or 2009. Terry was not committed to retirement because his financial goal was like a carrot at the end of the stick—elusive. As the years wore on, he always said he wanted just a bit more money in the bank first. I don't blame him: his store was doing really well, he had a strong management team in place, and he was in a new role as a director on the corporation's board. Things were pretty darn good. We planned on building on a lot that we had purchased late in September of 2005, but we didn't have a timeline. Now was not the time to worry about our future.

By the time the shuttle arrived, Terry looked a little nervous. If he did have a sense of impending doom, he never expressed any concern to me. I just know that when we arrived at the tiny airport, we were the first ones there. Our plane, sitting out on the tarmac, didn't resemble the aircraft that had brought us here. Terry was very quiet, possibly even anxious. Whether he sensed something or was just starting to gear up for work again, I didn't, and will never, know.

Eventually all the other passengers arrived. Two ladies about my age and their small dog entered the arrivals area, as well as a mom and dad and their two small children. I boarded the small plane first and quickly surveyed the seating situation. It was a one-and-two: one seat on the left of the aisle, two on the right. Because Terry had a sore left knee, I quickly decided to sit alone in the single left hand seat immediately behind the pilot, thereby allowing Terry to sit where he could stretch his left leg into the (admittedly small) aisle. Without our discussing it, he chose exactly as I intended. The passengers didn't really make contact with each other as we all chose our seats. The pilot strapped himself in, and after what seemed like an unusually long time, he eventually radioed for takeoff.

Terry was a man who was as solid as the rock he perched himself on less than twenty-four hours before his untimely death. He was a self-made man, having come from humble beginnings. His father was a fur-trapper who drove a school bus, while his mother styled and cut hair from their home. They basically ate what they could grow, can, or hunt. His life on the farm back in Bancroft, Ontario, was simple, full and very close to nature. I say this because, while Terry's childhood may have been simple, he was a driven adult who worked his butt off to get himself into engineering school. He partied hard back then and he worked even harder. He always managed to get top grades despite his active social life.

Terry married young, at twenty-two, and while his marriage lasted twenty-four years to the mother of his two sons, Craig and Kevin, he was not very happy from the very start. It was over the next twenty years that Terry developed his many passions like scuba diving, skiing, salmon fishing, bird hunting, running, golfing, and more. He was also not happy working for somebody else. He had the drive and ambition to be his own boss, which he finally achieved in his mid-thirties.

Terry learned to substitute activity for love. His driving personality pushed him to excel at everything he did. He later admitted to me that what he lacked in his marriage, he initially found in numerous loveless affairs. Admittedly, he looked outside to fill the void he felt inside as well.

I write about this not to disparage Terry's character by any stretch of the imagination. The truth was, I was looking in the mirror myself when I finally met Terry, as I too had taken the exact same path. Like attracts like. We kept searching and searching for love ... just all in the wrong places. I know that Terry and I were faithful to each other. We finally met our matches. We each challenged and excited each other at the same time.

Our last few days together were... perfect. I couldn't have planned it any better and I am just so thankful that we were able to enjoy some alone time together. So if it had to be this way and it did, then I am just so thankful we loved each other that week and we had no unfinished business between us.

Just learning to walk

Posing with pigtails and purse

Standing out from my friends

Mom and Me – my scowl says it all

Twit, Twit, Twoo, - A joyful Jilly

Luxury bucket shower in Delhi, India

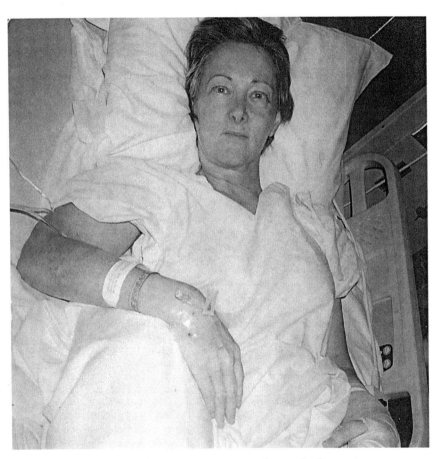

Pillows and percocet got me through the pain

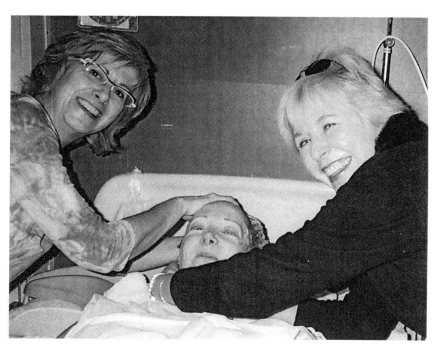

My first shampoo - Laurie, me and Eileen

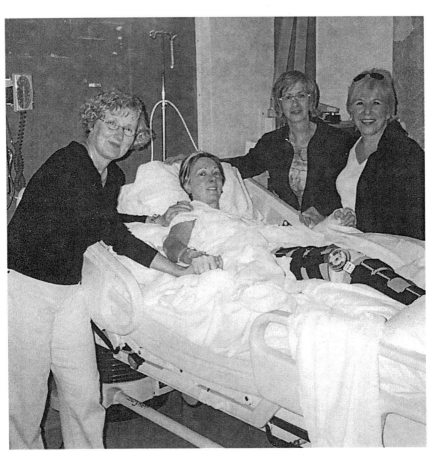

Awaiting back surgery - Lois, me, Laurie, and Eileen

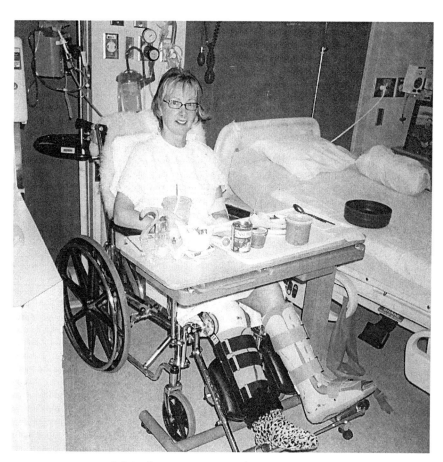

A big day siting up after one month

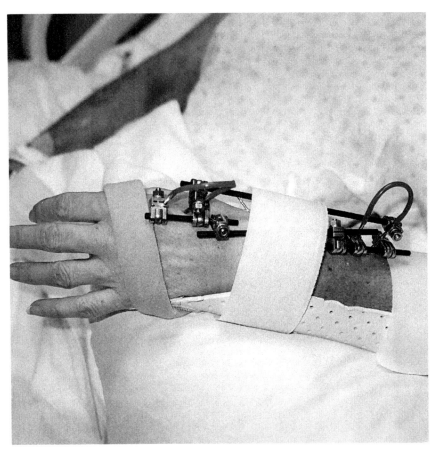

Burns, bruises and apparatuses

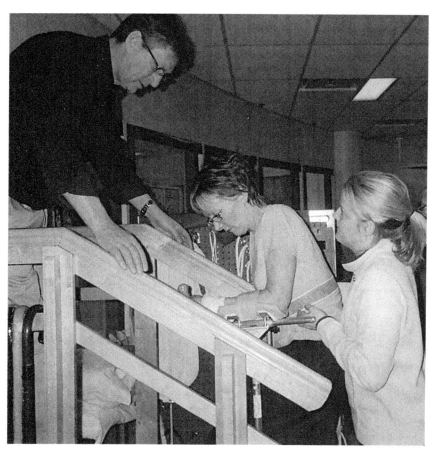

Brian, me and nurse attempting stairs for the first time

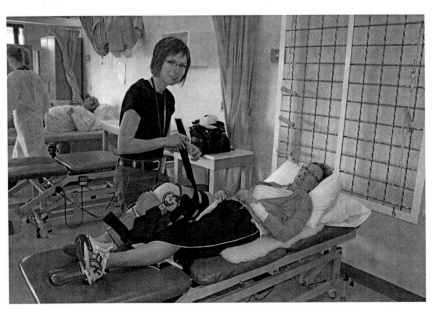

Measuring my progress in rehab

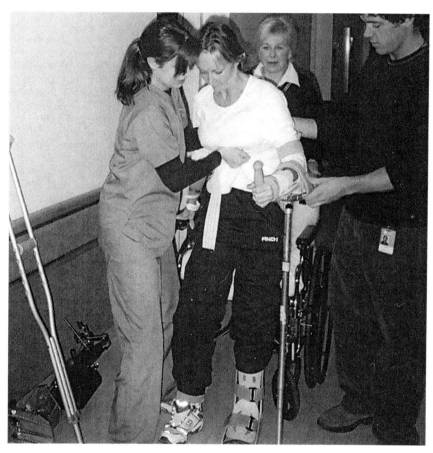

Preparing to walk with all my apparatuses

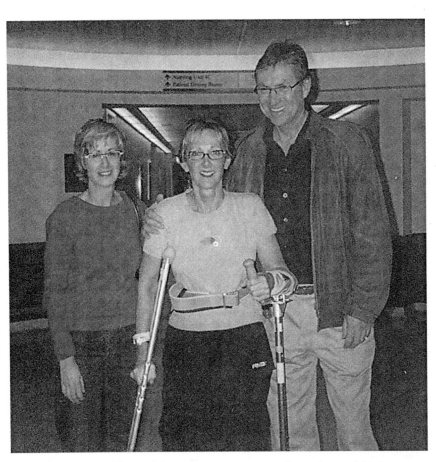

Walking with my biggest supporters – Laurie and Brian

"There are only two ways to live your life.
One is as though nothing is a miracle.
The other is as if everything is."

Albert Einstein

Part Three: Rescue and Recovery

Chapter Fourteen—The Miraculous Rescue

I regained consciousness, dazed and disoriented, a couple of minutes after we crashed. I found my left foot dangling outside of the plane, clearly broken and starting to swell. My shoe felt extremely tight, and my foot was pointing in the wrong direction. At the time, I remembered being bewildered at how the force of my left foot could have possibly made a hole in the side of the plane... but it did. I now felt the coldness of the mountain air as I could see bright white snow just beyond my dangling left foot. The front of my head had a deep gash from which blood poured. I felt a sense of confusion and total disbelief. When I finally remembered to look at my watch, it was 2:15; I was probably unconscious for about five minutes.

I could see and just barely touch Terry's left elbow. Debris covered the rest of his body. I knew he was dead, but I kept trying to nudge him awake, hoping beyond hope that he was simply unconscious. I couldn't wrap my head around what had happened, couldn't believe that my husband was gone. However, due to the angle that the plane crashed into the mountain, it would have been a true miracle for him to survive: the death certificate would state Terry's cause of death as blunt force trauma to the chest.

Unable to move an inch, I became keenly aware of the eerie

mountain silence outside the plane. Inside the remains of the fuselage I could hear moaning and groaning. From my vantage point, I couldn't see anything behind me. I was jammed into the pilot's seat right in front of me, which constricted my ability to move or turn in any direction. I lay in that uncomfortable position waiting for the next miracle to occur, the first being that I had survived!

One of the two ladies from the back of the plane was literally hanging precariously above me, so we could converse. She was aware that at least one of her legs was broken, which prevented her from moving around as well. We wondered if we could call somebody using my cell phone, tucked in my purse nearby. Then I remembered with dread that I had decided to put the phone in my luggage just before we boarded.

I heard her calling out to her partner, originally at the back of the plane, but now crumpled right behind me, to keep awake and to keep breathing. I gathered she was fading in and out of consciousness. None of us had known each other before the flight took off from Tofino airport; now this tragedy was about to bring us together in a way that we could never have imagined.

As reality set in, I asked if she could assist me by undoing the shoulder strap that was binding me rather tightly and making it difficult to breathe. My right arm was free, but my right knee was severely bent and pushed into my torso making it impossible to reach the release buckle. My left wrist was broken and beginning to swell, which rendered that hand useless. She was able to release the buckle, making it easier for me to breathe with what I thought might be a collapsed lung.

We remained like this for about an hour and a quarter, when I finally heard the whirring sounds of the rescue helicopter's approach. Luckily for us, the Canadian Search and Rescue Squadron (SARS) happened to be in the area that day and received the mayday calls from our pilot; although it was like finding a needle in a haystack, they located us just in the nick of time. I thanked God and let out a sigh of relief. The wait seemed like an eternity when faced with the uncertainly of whether any of us who survived the initial impact would live or die. The terrible fear that we all might be blown to bits if the airplane exploded occupied my mind, since the stench of the airplane fuel that was pouring all over me could easily have ignited. Also, not knowing if anyone would find us before we bled, froze, or burned to death was almost as horrific as the crash itself.

I could hear the rescue team call out to each other as they circled the plane on foot, trying to ascertain what the conditions were at the crash site. I heard someone say that there were two black and four red; I quickly surmised that was rescue speak for two dead and four alive. They hadn't discovered the two small children underneath Terry or me yet. The little boy was hidden from view near Terry, and was later discovered dead. The little girl was pinned underneath me, whimpering—which at least meant she was alive. Their mother lay out of my sightline, and for the most part, she remained quiet while the rescue team spent several minutes trying to stabilize her.

As for me, I felt fairly calm, since I didn't have much pain. Our bodies are amazing when it comes to trauma: the adrenaline flows and all other systems that are not needed for absolute survival simply shut down or at least defer to what is essential to survival. Shock keeps tremendous pain at bay. That's the good news.

When I thought about Terry, I couldn't even cry; I could only whimper. Oddly enough, I remember thinking, *Lucky Terry. Now he knows what it's like to be on the other side.* At the same time, though, inside my head, I was desperately pleading with the rescue team, *you don't understand—that's my husband, you must save him!* As if to answer my silent pleas, they checked Terry again, but seemingly spent very little time on him, whereas they continued to recheck the pilot's pulse over and over. I knew why. The pilot had survived initially, but I saw him take his last breath, and slump peacefully over the stick, mere minutes before the rescue team arrived. The pilot was probably still warm, while Terry had been dead for over ninety minutes.

Several more minutes passed before one of the members of the rescue team suddenly realized that the liquid pouring on me was in fact airplane fuel. He called frantically to the others to stop all cutting. They had started to use a chainsaw to hack away at the airplane parts that prevented them from freeing us from our metal prisons; a single spark would have instantly ignited the fuel, creating an inferno. In the end, I was the only passenger who sustained head-to-toe second-degree burns from the fuel.

That morning I had been first on the plane; now I was the last survivor taken out of the wreckage. They had used all the stretchers to evacuate the other three ladies and little girl; so two young men gathered me up under my arms and literally had to *clunk* me over the tops of the crumpled guts of the plane. I could feel my legs and feet, but I had no strength to lift myself. I was like a ragdoll in their arms.

Ironically, the onset of hypothermia represented more good news for all of us: lowering body temperature in the injured increases the chances of survival. My teeth may have been chattering away, but I tried to remain calm and very conscious of trying to do my yoga breathing. After they removed me from the plane, I remained lying in the snow for probably over an hour, completely gas soaked and with very little clothing on. It was hard to breathe, but still I didn't panic. Occasionally, one of the young rescuers would come by to check on and comfort me. He would reassure me that I was going to be okay and to hang in there, and then off he'd go to assist the other survivors. I couldn't see where they placed anyone else, but I knew no one was close to me, at maybe seventy-five yards away from the crash site.

My mind kept racing, thinking, *What about Terry?* I knew he was dead; I just didn't want it to be true. I wanted to ask the team, "Could you check him one more time?" The thought of leaving my husband behind in the middle of winter, thinking he was dead when maybe he was just unconscious … I couldn't get any further with those thoughts. It was unfathomable.

The rain that day had created a thin crust on top of the snow, making the area far too unstable to land the large rescue helicopter. So once all the survivors were extricated from the plane, they now had to determine how to maneuver each of us onto this massive, hovering helicopter.

As time wore on, I began to feel the pain of my injuries fully. I knew I had broken-bone pain, but more obvious and immediate was the soft-tissue pain. At this point I only knew my left ankle and left wrist were broken; I hadn't yet discovered my back was fractured, or realized any of the myriad other injuries I'd sustained. I knew I wasn't paralyzed, which was a relief. Finally, a good four to five hours after the crash, I felt myself being loaded into the helicopter. We were finally on our way to the hospital.

Another thirty minutes and none of us would have made it out alive, as temperatures on the mountain were quickly plummeting to below zero. After nightfall, we would have been forced to spend the whole night on the mountain because of poor visibility for the helicopter pilots. None of us would have survived our injuries.

Reality sank in. Just hours earlier, Terry and I were ending our romantic getaway —now this! "Oh, God," I cried, "What just happened?"

The helicopter touched down on the tarmac near St. Joseph's Hospital in Comox, and we were all rushed to the tiny emergency room. I don't know what happened, really; I remember waking up to my clothes being cut off by a nurse and a team of doctors prodding me all over and asking me numerous questions: "Can you feel this?" "Are you sore here?" I later learned I had been barely clinging to life. At some point I was given six liters of blood. For those three or more hours, they were simply trying to stabilize me.

Amid the chaos, another nurse came in with a phone and asked me if I wanted to call someone. *Oh my God, my family!* The only two numbers that I could recall were my mom's and my best friend Laurie's, back home in St. Albert. The nurse kindly called my mom. Upon hearing her voice, I could tell immediately she was in a state of shock. I could hear her relief at finally hearing my voice. For some reason I simply said, "I think Terry is gone." *Gone where?* I wondered as I said it. I had never before been in this situation where I had to give the news that someone in our family had died. That's just what came out of my mouth.

"Dead" was too harsh and too real. I didn't think my mom could handle it. I wasn't sure I was handling it, frankly. I told her I was a little banged up, but I was fine. At that point, I really couldn't comprehend all my injuries. "Don't worry about me," I said, even though I was about to go in for some surgery. The nurses spelled out for my mom what was really going on. My parents and my brother and his wife hurried to catch the ferry first thing the next morning in order to get to the hospital to see me. Obviously, I was not fine!

In the meantime, my good old dad (as he likes to call himself) was supposed to pick us up from the airport. He always volunteered to do almost anything we asked of him, but had a tendency to get dates, times, and/or locations mixed up, so when we didn't show up at the designated time, he hadn't been sure what to think. Apparently, the personnel from the airline hadn't been forthcoming with the details of the accident, and so Dad didn't learn about the crash until much later that evening. Family members who were picking up the passengers that day were sent home with no real news. Sonic Blue's representatives didn't mention the crash.

I later found out that my dad had made several urgent phone calls to my brother Steve in North Vancouver, who quickly got online and put two and two together. That started their frantic calls to the Royal Canadian Mounted Police, (RCMP) and the hospitals on the island. Due to privacy laws, they weren't revealing names, but my brother could conclude that I must be injured; it wasn't like me *not* to phone if plans had changed.

Eight hours of uncertainty and worry passed for my family before Mom called and said she had talked to me, although she couldn't recount anything I'd said, except the essential news that I was alive. My parents were in their late seventies, with my mom in the early stages of dementia, so this was difficult and very emotional for both of them. They were all stunned to hear of Terry's death. To everyone who knew him, Terry was invincible.

My second call went to my best friend, Laurie, in St. Albert. She and her husband Brian had just stepped in the door from a concert when the phone rang. I heard a shocked response to my extremely weak voice saying, "Hello, Laurie?"

This time I was able to say that Terry had died. I could feel her concern and compassion for me, and her shock over Terry's passing. I then asked her if she could go to our house and walk the dogs. By now we had two more Springer's, Drake and Reba (Duffy had died a couple of years earlier). They'd been left in their cages alone for a good twelve hours by now. I had forgotten that one of Terry's managers was staying at our house to take care of Reba and Drake. I didn't ask Laurie about the next day; I was only thinking about that day, as if somehow I would be there tomorrow to walk them.

I don't remember much else that I told Laurie, but by now, the doctors had found something on me that *did* hurt and were indicating that they would take the phone now. I remember the very odd feeling of talking on the phone and at the same time I could literally feel my skull closing stitch by stitch. I said good-bye, and after that, I don't recall anything else I said. A short while later, I was being prepped for the first of many surgeries I would have over the next three years.

I didn't have any opportunity to call Terry's sons, Kevin and Craig, or his sister, Lois and brother-in-law Jim. I later found out that the RCMP made all the necessary phone calls.

It turned out that the lady (Melissa) hanging above me on the plane stayed in Comox, as did I. There we each had the initial operations to stabilize our conditions. The little girl was flown to Children's Hospital in Vancouver, while her mother and the other lady (Stacey) were sent to the Victoria Hospital. Their recovery was made that much more difficult because now the two different families were separated. After they stabilized me, doctors determined that I should make my full recovery in Alberta. There was some red tape to go through, but by Wednesday, a mere five days later, I was heavily sedated and put back on a plane headed for the University of Alberta Hospital. My sister-in-law, Lois, accompanied me

Needless to say, Kevin and Lois were both in their own states of shock. Kevin and his dad had been quite close; hearing the devastating news from an Ontario police officer in the early hours of Sunday morning was not how either of them would have chosen to share the news. As I headed back to Alberta with Lois, I had a moment of survivor's guilt: I should have been the one to die, not Terry. I wanted to comfort Kevin and say I was sorry, as if I was somehow responsible for the plane crash. Instead, he arrived a few days later with a large eight-by-ten photo of the last picture I had taken of Terry on the rocks near the Wickaninnish Inn.

The camera was found among all the passengers' belongings, which were brought to a hangar several days later for the survivors' families to sift through. Kevin found our camera, which was toast, but he was able to recover the card. We had a tender moment of shared grief, despite my broken parts. It was then I knew Kevin's and Craig's lives had also changed forever. I struggled to keep my composure for Kevin, as if to somehow shield him from any more pain.

Chapter Fifteen—The Transition Home to Edmonton

At St. Joseph's, they'd told me that the rescue team had camped overnight at the crash site with the two remaining dead bodies: the pilot and Terry. I was later told that they were protecting a potential crime scene, just in case foul play was involved. Even though the little boy had also died at the crash site, the rescue team decided to take his body on the helicopter.

Because of the cold and the delay between his death and the team's arrival, I had no doubt they would had to have cut Terry's body apart to remove him from the plane. So I suggested that Terry's body be cremated in Comox and his ashes sent to Edmonton. I didn't want to deny Kevin and Craig their chance to say goodbye to their father, but under the circumstances it would be best if they remembered Terry as the vibrant, strong man that he was. We would deal with his service at a later time.

Leaving Comox was easier after I made the hard decision of what to do with Terry's remains, as well as determining that Lois would accompany me back home to Edmonton. We bid a tearful farewell to the ICU nurses. I would be forever grateful for their loving care and attention to my every need. I was very thankful that at least I could go home and start on my way to recovery.

We arrived in Edmonton just before midnight on Wednesday evening, January 26. Recovering in my hometown meant I would be close to friends and family who could assist me in the many ways I would inevitably need. The flight on the special medical plane took approximately ninety minutes. Although I wasn't really cognizant of it, thanks to the sedation, people who were very attentive to all of my needs once again surrounded me. It's actually a wonder I remember anything, but flying in another small plane so soon after the crash kept me on full alert. Fortunately, the time passed without incident. I trusted that a plane wouldn't crash twice. I told myself that the universe and God don't work like that.

I'll show everyone, I thought. *I'll be out of the hospital and back home in a couple of days.*

The male admitting nurse at the University of Alberta Hospital in Edmonton reminded me of Drake Amore, a doctor from a soap opera played by the character Joey in his job as an actor on the sitcom *Friends*. The nurse was completely bald, looked really young, and wore an earring in one ear. His name was Dirk—not that that has anything to do with the type of care he was giving me, but it did add a very small amount of humor for me at that rather bleak moment.

It turns out Dirk was very compassionate; he would slip over to my side of the ICU on his break to talk with me and show me pictures of his wife and three beautiful children on his iPod. This was a very small connection that spoke volumes to me in those moments of despair and sadness. My family and friends had downloaded some pictures to an iPod for me to look at and share with visitors in a desperate attempt to make me feel still connected.

I was glad that Dirk was very much a "take control" type person. As soon as I landed on the tarmac of the U of A hospital, he had nurses scurrying around me, doing exactly as he barked. He sounded like a drill sergeant, but somehow that comforted me in my new surroundings.

After the new team of doctors and nurses assessed me, I was immediately quarantined in ICU. Everyone, including visitors, had to wear gowns and masks merely to come near me. Because I had come from another province, they needed to ensure I didn't cause an outbreak. I felt comforted by these precautions and didn't mind the inconvenience at all.

However, I was soon to learn that to this new team, I was just another emergency. I didn't receive the round-the-clock care that I received at the Comox Hospital. For the first few days, my vitals were checked every hour, but eventually it became every four hours. Even when I was finally getting precious healing sleep, someone would come in and start checking my oxygen saturation, my blood pressure, etc. I found out later they were concerned about pneumonia setting in.

Nevertheless, I was at least home, in my city with my friends. Terry's cremated remains arrived more than a week after I did. Upon hearing that, I did breathe a sigh of relief. Even in his cremated state, I wanted to know that he was with me.

I had never broken a bone in my body prior to this and I had only been in the hospital for a few elective surgeries and the one ectopic pregnancy, so I didn't have much experience as a patient. I'd have thought I would have more of a say when it came to the plan of action, but I soon found out—just like anyone else who arrives at an emergency room—I had no say at all. Everything was pretty much decided for me. In the ICU, I received antianxiety drugs, sleeping pills, heavy painkillers, and anti-inflammatory agents. I was hooked up to oxygen and to an IV for fluids, and I had a catheter to hold the fluids I excreted. Despite the exhaustion and the sleeping pills, I only managed to sleep for maybe two hours a night. I was just so fearful that I might not wake up. For me, all this was unfathomable.

I was surprised to find out that the nurses in the ICU used their own money to provide toiletries like toothbrushes, toothpaste, and combs to new patients. Later that year, I took a large basket filled with shampoos, razors, toothbrushes, and more, to the unit to personally thank them for all they had done for me. It was quite the moment when they finally realized who I was, as of course by then I looked considerably different. I just wanted them to know I was grateful for and humbled by their service to their patients. It was my experience that their chosen profession teaches them compassion and allows them to see the human being behind the injuries.

Ironically during that visit, I was told that one of the young male nurses that looked after me and who was a friend of Kevin's had broken his own back while surfing in Tofino a few months after my stay. I remember cautioning him to be careful and not do anything crazy but to have fun with his girlfriend. When I heard of his injuries, I could only think that at least now he actually did know how it felt to have a broken back.

It was amazing to notice how my own sense of compassion had grown for anyone who used a wheel chair, had a slight limp, or possessed another obvious injury. I had previously judged people who seemed less than capable in my eyes. I was far too quick to judge a book by its cover. Now I realized I didn't have the right to judge anyone without knowing the whole story.

I also found out very quickly that doctors have giant egos. Unfortunately, when they attempted to assert their power over me, our egos clashed. I had to completely surrender to their choices of treatment. Looking back, I really wish I had been consulted more when it came to all my surgery decisions, particularly my back surgery, because I might have made different choices for myself than they did.

Fortunately, I had Lois, who is a nurse and very capable of standing up to doctors when they speak a language that most of us don't understand. In her incredibly loving and gentle way, she would ask them detailed questions, communicating clearly that they weren't going to pull the wool over her eyes. (Asking questions was crucial, not only of the doctors, but also of my accountants and lawyers who would later enter into the picture. Otherwise, everyone else would have control of my life and I would be left on the outside wondering what the heck was happening!) Thankfully, in the hospital, Lois was my advocate, and I completely trusted her.

On several occasions, we tussled with the doctors. They weren't used to being asked questions and they didn't like it. Somehow, I got the feeling that I should be bowing down to them for every little thing they said. It didn't seem to matter to them that I wanted them to know who I was and what this accident had taken from me. Did they have any idea that my husband was just killed? Of course they did, but that wasn't their concern. I needed compassion and understanding from them, but they just wanted to do their jobs.

I soon realized that I wasn't the only one they needed to care for. Code alerts popped up in the ICU all day long, which kept them all hopping. I finally came to terms with the real situation, and once we all got our egos acknowledged, we came to an understanding. I might add that my main orthopedic doctor brought me a box of chocolates on Valentine's Day, as his way of showing that he cared. And I must admit I was grateful for his expertise—he was an excellent orthopedic surgeon.

I was ordered flat on my back until the operation for my spinal fractures. They had to insert two five-inch metal rods on either side of my spine in the L1, L2, and T12 positions. The rods stayed in for over a year, inhibiting my movement and causing quite a bit of pain and discomfort. My decision to take them out was definitely the right thing to do, in spite of the fact it involved another operation and eight weeks of recovery and rehabilitation time.

It was even more frustrating that a year later, when I *could* have the rods removed, my case was no longer considered an emergency. This meant I would be put on the dreaded wait list. As anybody on that wait list can attest to, it can take a very long time before one is attended to—sometimes years! Fortunately for me, the squeaky wheel gets the grease, and I just kept squawking. I thank my doctor friends for expediting my case, because I know it would have been a much longer wait had they not intervened on my behalf.

I was scheduled for surgery on March 6, 2007, thirteen months after the original surgery. Still I had some anxiety wondering if my surgery would be bumped for an emergency, just like over a year earlier. After that, it still took over three years and semi-weekly trips to the chiropractor, rehab specialist, acupuncturist, osteopath, and massage therapist, before my back started to feel better for any length of time. All the parts have to be in working order for it to all heal harmoniously together. Unfortunately that was what made the physical part of my healing so hard and what took so long. All the major joints in my body were broken (left wrist, left ankle, left foot, right knee, right fibula, and spine) and even though they were now repaired, the real journey of healing begins with the surrounding muscles and soft tissues. Everything is connected!

All members of the surgical team did do their best, and for that I am grateful. I just had no idea how long the pain would last. In those moments that turned into years, I felt adrift, lost and emotionally unstable. My grieving process was just beginning.

On a more positive note, I learned humbleness, gratitude, and surrender very early, as so many of the nurses truly displayed a lot of compassion toward me. They did everything they could to try and make me more comfortable and to respect me as a person. When I did surrender, everyone simply became loving! As the well-known quote says, "When I changed how I perceived things, the things I perceived changed!"

Chapter Sixteen—My Team of Angels

I received my first hair wash several days after my arrival at the U of A hospital. Until then, I still had blood in my hair and underneath my manicure. How I looked was of little concern to anyone, even to me, but a simple thing like a hair wash gave me back some dignity and made me feel human again. My friends lovingly washed my hair with great care so as to not disturb my back, and finished off my day of beauty with a mini-manicure. Clean nails and hair gave me a reason to celebrate that day!

Nurses, doctors, friends, family, and even strangers took complete care of me. I couldn't do *anything* for myself. I couldn't feed myself, go to the bathroom, dress, sit up, or walk. I have always liked being in control, so surrendering didn't come naturally, but in my new, shattered state, it was easy to let go! I didn't have any other choice.

Every broken body part rested atop a pillow for some comfort. The nurses would roll me over like a log, every few hours, to relieve my pain. This required a minimum of two nurses; sometimes four depending on who was on duty, for they had to ensure my spine wasn't inadvertently bumped.

I was hooked up to a catheter for my nearly three-week stay at the University of Alberta hospital. Near the end of my stint there,

I contracted a bladder infection, making urination very painful. Fortunately, they were able to eradicate the infection quickly, and when I did finally empty my bladder, the nurse could only exclaim "You really did have to go!"

There is no privacy when it comes to your body in a hospital, and thus I also learned humility. The support staff was just doing their jobs and I might say, doing it well. I remember the night a nurse came in to clean me *down there*. She was horrified at the burns I had received and, rather uncharacteristically, showed it. I sensed she was equally as horrified that I hadn't been washed in my private parts yet. I was getting sponge baths in bed, if not every day then every other day, but they had neglected to go there. It was of little concern to me, as most of my thinking time was spent dealing with the pain. I hadn't yet had a bowel movement thanks to the anesthesia, but what a relief when it did finally come some eight days after the accident.

Early on, I was focused on the number fifteen. Every fifteen minutes I could press the button that was my link to my morphine drip. Ah, relief. The pain was excruciating, but the morphine masked it beautifully. After about two weeks of morphine use, I started to recognize that I was hallucinating during the night. The constant whirring sounds of all the machines played a symphony with other weird sounds that my drug-addled mind created. I had nightmares in which someone was trying to kill me. I expressed my concerns to the nurse, who took me seriously. They stopped the morphine drip and put me on Percocet, which is a very strong, addictive painkiller.

Now I was focused on the number four. I was allowed two Percocet every four hours. That was twelve per day. For most people, one pill would make their head spin; for me, however, it barely hid the pain. They hesitated to give me more, because of the addictive qualities, but the nurses were very insistent that I stay ahead of the pain. Despite my dislike for taking drugs, I didn't argue one bit about taking whatever they would give me to kill the pain. Most of the time I wasn't coherent, and I certainly couldn't put words, let alone sentences, together. I felt spaced out and completely helpless to do anything about it.

Meanwhile, back at the ranch, my home and my two dogs were being tended to. Laurie took it upon herself to organize all my friends into what I lovingly refer to as my team of angels. Quickly my new team adjusted their busy lives and schedules to include taking care of the countless details involving my dogs, Terry's death, and me. They even helped take care of Terry's Canadian Tire store with its 130 employees who were in complete shock after losing their friend and their wonderful boss.

My friends desperately wanted to visit me in the hospital and to do *something* to take away even a little bit of my pain. Unfortunately, I was in no shape to see many people, at least not yet. Every night, after spending hours with me, Laurie would go home and update everyone on the latest news that day. Any news was good news to my friends, and I was so happy at having Laurie there for me.

I can assure you that so many people were pitching in to try and assist me that I probably don't even know the half of it. I learned one thing from this experience: the people who truly love and care for you want to do anything they can to help you when you need it the most. And for all of that, I just felt extremely grateful.

I won't bore you with the details of each surgery, except to say that each one was another moment in time when I wondered if I'd make it through. My thoughts always ran, *If I could survive a plane crash, I can survive a mere three-hour operation*, or, *Please God, let me get through just this one, then the next one!* An infection set into my right knee, which necessitated two more surgeries, first to scope it and then to clean the insides and repair the damage.

Some days, I was consumed with anxiety. Looking back, I can definitely see why I needed the antianxiety medications: there were a whole lot of balls in the air and someone had to juggle them, but this time it couldn't be me. It was especially difficult for me, as the one with the perfect princess life, to surrender to the possibility that some of the balls might fall and there was nothing I could do about it. Grieving for my many losses, especially for Terry, would not even come about for at least another nine months.

I had six operations in a matter of two weeks and a total of eleven surgeries over a three-and-a-half-year period. Each surgery involved not eating or drinking for twelve hours or more prior to surgery. At least twice, my scheduled operation was cancelled at the last moment, leaving me hungry and very weak … and having to surrender to it all.

The hospital food was, not surprisingly, less than nutritious. Before the accident, I had adhered to a high-protein diet and limited my white carbohydrates. Hospital meals were mostly simple carbohydrates with very little protein. Predictably, food often arrived cold and, to make matters worse was left at the foot of my bed; for a patient who is immobile, that's very frustrating. Fortunately, this sparked my team of angels to come up with a solution. With the exception of breakfasts, they cooked and delivered every other meal. Despite the medication-induced nausea, I tried my best to eat everything put in front of me because it was made with pure love. In all, I lost twenty-three pounds and was down to a mere 107 when I finally got home. I was a skeleton of my former self. When I could finally look in the mirror, I was shocked and devastated. I looked so weak and frail; most of my muscle mass had atrophied. For whatever reason, my thyroid was in overdrive, so whatever I was able to keep down wasn't enough to keep the weight on. Despite the fact that I was doing absolutely nothing but lying around all day, I was wasting away

I was in no position to visit with everybody except the select few who were my core team. I couldn't possibly face every new person and recount the story that I had told dozens of times by now. It was just too painful and I was still very fragile. Yet every day I would receive wonderful bouquets of flowers and very thoughtful cards from people just trying to connect and express their love to me. I was very touched by it all. In fact it overwhelmed me ... in a positive way. All of those cards, flowers, and e-mails definitely boosted my desire to get better. Linda, my India hiking partner, put together the Flower Power people. Every week for long past my stay at this hospital I would receive a wonderful new bouquet of flowers that certainly brightened my week. In fact, I looked forward to it, as it was a reminder that I wasn't forgotten

Another vital part of my team was Lois, Terry's sister. Lois, who lived in Kingston, took time off from her job as a neonatal nurse in the Kingston General Hospital just to care for me. Every day for three weeks straight, Laurie and Lois sat by my bedside and either listened to me talk or just sat quietly giving me their love and support. At no time did I feel alone. Even though I was slurring my words and it took great effort to put sentences together, I was a chatty Cathy. I had so much to say and I just needed to get it out. Often they would they would rub my burnt skin with a soothing lotion. The hospital staff was amazed at how quickly my burns were healing. I knew why. It was the love and lotion combo that did it. In fact, it was at least two weeks before I had a moment to myself an afternoon just to sleep and rest. By this time, Laurie and Lois badly needed the reprieve as well.

I remember thinking during that alone time that I had two choices to make. I could go down the road of despair, or I could go down the road of uncertainty. The latter held the unknown, but at the same time, I knew it would be better than the unthinkable road of despair. Somehow, I knew from the moment we crashed there must be a much bigger reason for my surviving. I just didn't have any idea what it could be yet. I chose to accept what is is. After all, I wasn't dead, I wasn't paralyzed, I wasn't in a coma, and I wasn't brain damaged. I saw no other real option; I simply chose the road of uncertainty and remained positive. Everyone else around me was acting so positive and was always so encouraging ... why shouldn't I believe in my recovery?

So I did. In fact, I saw the beauty in it. I was most grateful to every little act of kindness that anyone showed me, from the cleaning lady who emptied my trash, to the nurses who changed my bedpans. They all seemed to exude kindness and compassion. Sure, there were sorrowful times, but for the most part, their constant love and support went a long way in making me believe that there was light at the end of the long, dark tunnel.

Almost a month after the crash, I was able to sit up for the first time. The first attempt I made to sit up left me completely drenched in a cold sweat. My legs dangled over the sides of my bed and quivered uncontrollably. Just that effort alone took about thirty minutes, after which I collapsed back onto my bed, exhausted. I sheepishly looked at the nurses and asked them if I could try again the next day.

The next day came too soon, and once again I trembled as the sweat beaded on my forehead. I refused to quit, and eventually I was able to take my first few steps to the bathroom. Once I got there I discovered that I couldn't bend by myself in order to sit down. I was so stiff that my body literally wouldn't bend. With assistance from the nurses I did manage to sit down on the raised toilet seat. Every little movement in the upright position resulted in severe pain. Even though the intention was for me to use the toilet, I wasn't able to concentrate enough to do anything.

On February 17, 2006, nearly a month after the crash, I was transferred to the Glenrose Rehabilitation Hospital in Edmonton. I had had all the surgeries necessary, or so they thought at that time, and I was no longer considered an intensive care patient. Once they had gotten me sitting up and walking, even though it was a feeble attempt, my attending doctors thought I would be better served in a rehabilitation hospital.

However, this move proved to be a misstep for me. Eighteen months later, another doctor in Vancouver who specialized in feet confirmed that my left foot had been broken in the crash, but had been overlooked during my original diagnosis. My attempts to walk and recover from my other surgeries (back, wrist, ankle, and knee) were impeding my full recovery. Unfortunately for me, there were so many other parts that hurt equally as much; I didn't realize how painful my foot was. Now, it became apparent that although the bones in my left foot had already healed, they weren't in the right place for me to ever walk comfortably again.

Of course, none of that mattered to me at the moment I finally stood upright. It had finally clicked for me this wasn't exactly going to be easy. Yes, all the broken parts were supposedly fixed, but how about the excruciating body pain? Just lying in bed and taking pain medication was a whole lot different than actually having to move, let alone function in life again all by myself. My physio and occupational therapists, however, remained very encouraging.

I recalled the conversation I had with the initial doctor in Comox, who performed my wrist and ankle surgeries. I asked him how long he thought it would take me to recover, suggesting, "You think by April?" A good three months away seemed like forever. He slowly shook his head, so I asked, "June?"

Again he shook his head.

Thinking I was being overly cautious, I ventured, "August?"

At that point he could probably tell that I had no clue as to the extent of my injuries, and it would be best if he didn't tell me any specific length of time. I wish he had, because I had no idea it would take the better part of four years.

However, true to my character, I firmly believed that he just didn't know me—as though I were somehow special or different and could recover much more quickly than he anticipated. Oh, how humbled I would become!

Chapter Seventeen—Simplify: Every Day is a Diamond Day

Before the accident, I would never have been able to say I possessed strengths such as courage, patience, or perseverance. My friends would tell me during my recovery that I had all those qualities and more. I realized that they interpreted the fact that I had to surrender to so many other people (who had complete control of my life at the moment) as me being patient.

I should have accepted their praise graciously. Instead, I really wanted to shout at them that I didn't want to be strong and courageous; I simply wanted my life back–it had been perfect, remember?

When I finally faced my new reality, all I could see was myself lying in the snow waiting to be rescued, my body broken and in shock, and my beloved husband gone forever. I knew at that moment that my life would never be the same.

I had to get used to many significant changes in my life. I also knew I had to find the new me: a forty-seven-year-old widow who was broken physically, emotionally, and mentally, but certainly not spiritually. I would soon find out that the spiritual side was about to blossom. My faith was going to be tested in ways I couldn't have imagined. Cataclysmic events are often followed by major transformations, at

138

least according to Bruce Lipton, author of *Spontaneous Evolution*. The transformation was beginning and the new and improved Jilly was emerging. I grew proud of my war wounds and scars. They were my badges of honor.

Prior to this life-altering experience, I would have described my life as pretty darn fantastic. Of course, that was because my ego mind saw myself as being very fit; I had my own flourishing and satisfying interior design business; I had a very hard-working, successful, loving, and faithful husband. Our successes allowed us to live in a beautifully appointed, spacious home on acreage in the country, to drive luxury cars, and to vacation about eight to twelve weeks per year. Our lifestyle was certainly one of ease and comfort. In my mind, we had it all. Make no mistake—Terry and I both worked really hard to achieve this. We were finally reaching a pinnacle of success that we both had dreamed about all our lives.

Not that there is anything wrong with material success, but when faced with life and death, material accomplishments took a backseat to my concerns for family and friends, and the experiences that we once shared.

Terry's boys were doing well. At the time, the younger, Kevin, age thirty, was enrolled in the MBA program at the Rothman School of Business in Toronto. The elder, Craig, thirty-two, was employed at the Black Dog, a local bar in the trendy part of Edmonton known as Old Strathcona. Both were stable. Our wide circle of equally successful friends hailed mostly from Terry's fraternity of the Canadian Tire Dealers' Association. His recent appointment as a member of the Board of Directors on the Canadian Tire Corporate Board was an honor after a long and varied career as a successful dealer, with stores in Meaford, ON; Fort Saskatchewan, AB; and finally, his last store in St. Albert, AB. We were happy in friends, family, and work. In fact, the Christmas before the plane crash, Terry had surprised me with an eye popping three-and-a-half-carat diamond ring. Terry was reluctant to spend money on something as frivolous as diamonds, but he knew I found jewelry important and meaningful. This was a for sure sign he loved me.

I've always loved diamonds. My philosophy on life stated that every day is a diamond day. This viewpoint came from my mom, not because she had them, but because she didn't. She may have wanted some, but her family was her priority. Instead, I remember distinctly as a little girl, being told that my only dress that hung in my closet was my good dress that I could only wear on special occasions. Unfortunately by the time a special occasion came around, I had outgrown it. I never got to wear that beautiful pink dress with the empire waist and white satin bow. That left a lasting impression on me. In my adult years, I translated that one childhood experience to my personal mantra. Why wait for that special occasion? If you can afford it, wear your diamonds every day. After the crash, of course, I'd have easily given up my diamond days just to have my husband and my old life back. Still, I hung onto the concept, because you just never know when it will be your last day.

Because of my injuries I held a "Celebration of Life" for Terry almost four months after his death. I can't thank everyone enough for their patience in waiting to pay their own respects to their good friend. It took me over two months just to plan Terry's celebration, with tremendous help from my team of angels. My friend Beverlee lovingly put together a montage of pictures and music.

May 11 was the same day as the Canadian Tire Shareholders meeting in Toronto, and so some of his fellow Board members were not able to attend—which honestly didn't make me sad. In fact, it was somewhat fortuitous, as I didn't want the ceremony to be only about Canadian Tire. Terry was my husband, my lover, and my friend … the man I wanted to grow old with. I feared that some people might try and take over and make this celebration only about being a Canadian Tire dealer. He was obviously so much more to me.

At the same time, as I was co-executor of Terry's will, I also had to deal with the insurance companies and the Canadian Tire Corporation for the sale of Terry's store. The insured families were supposed to be looked after immediately after a dealer's death. Well, not so much for me! I fell through the cracks somehow, and when I finally asked the question as to what was happening with Terry's case (sometime in April after I returned from the Glenrose Hospital), the Dealer's Association realized that the person who was supposed to be handling it thought someone else had already handled it. In the end, no one was handling it.

My friend Shirley, another angel on my team and a dealer's wife from Vancouver, was of great assistance to me. She was familiar with the organization and wasn't afraid to get on the phone and ask the questions. They were apologetic, but that didn't excuse this situation. Really, if the slogan of the Canadian Tire Foundation is *Helping Families When They Need It Most*, why weren't they helping the wife of one of their very own board members? I realized the truth that business must go on. To me, it was our life, my life … but to them it was just a blip! I think even Terry would have been shocked as to how I was treated after he had dedicated his time and life to Canadian Tire. I felt completely abandoned.

I could have a bad taste in my mouth for very valid reasons, but in the end I let go of that as well. I knew this chapter of my life was over. It wasn't really even my life; it was Terry's life. Why should I hold on to anger over something that wasn't even mine? I have long since forgiven them for their lack of support. I have concluded that perhaps losing Terry was such a shock to them as well, that they honestly forgot to follow through with their responsibilities regarding his family.

At the same time, Terry had another insurance policy. He had explained to me a few months before the crash that the other policy carried double indemnity. Therefore, in the case of an accident, the policy would be worth double the amount for which it was written. I had sat mostly in silence that Sunday afternoon as he went over the details of our financial life to be sure I understood everything. I did, but I couldn't help but wonder why he was bringing this up at this time. I still really wonder if he had a premonition of his own death.

While I was in the hospital, no one was following up with the other insurance policy. When I finally did get to speak to someone in person, some four months after the crash, the first thing they told me was that the delay in payment was caused by some questions they had about the cause. I listened with growing fury as they asked whether Terry had piloted the plane, flying a suicide mission, or if he might have had a heart attack prior to the crash and thus died before the accident even took place. These were their excuses for not having to pay anything out yet. Despite my weakness from my injuries, these statements got my blood boiling—I would not back down.

Finally in June, six months after the crash and several frustrating discussions with several insurance agents (I could never get the same one to talk to me), they finally agreed I had a valid claim. I half believe that they only agreed to pay at that time because I had e-mailed them a copy of the *Toronto Star* article in which it clearly reported that this was a commercial flight, with other passengers unknown to us prior to the flight, and that Terry's cause of death was blunt force trauma to his chest.

By that time, there was an investigation as to the cause of the sudden loud bang and the engine failure. The airline involved was and had been under close scrutiny by Transport Canada for errors in several categories involving maintenance of their small fleet of planes for quite some time.

Two things became apparent to me. First, the companies' stalling tactics were hampering my recovery, both physically and emotionally. Second, now that I was the one left in charge of this mess, I had to be my own advocate. I was dealing with doctors, lawyers, accountants, financial advisers, and trust officers. As co-executor of Terry's will, which had set up four trusts of which I was both an executor and a beneficiary, I found myself dealing with another conflict of interest. All in all, there were far too many balls in the air; some were beginning to drop.

Equally clear was the fact that I had no choice but to go through all these hoops, just when I wanted to simplify my life and take time to just heal. I became even more determined to recover as quickly as possible just so I could be capable and clear-headed. I needed to take charge of my whole self without the interference of the mind-altering drugs. I needed to ask all the right questions of the so-called experts who were directing my life in a way that wasn't what I wanted, nor what Terry and I had intended.

I knew what Terry had told me was true and the insurance companies were simply trying to wear me down. They didn't know that Terry had been very upfront with me about all his financial dealings; my impression was that they thought I was "just the wife." That may sound odd, but I know of many close female friends who knew little to nothing about their real financial situation. This was a truth; it just wasn't my truth.

So while the frustration and stress did take their toll on my health, it turned out to be a very positive experience, because it forced me to be capable far beyond my own expectations of what I could do. I hadn't yet learned that I was working with those subconscious limiting beliefs that said, *I am not worthy, I am not capable,* or *I'm just a girl and I can't handle such complicated matters.* Fortunately for me, on a conscious level I knew I had to step up and perform like always—only this time it was for me and in Terry's honor.

In later years, my therapist explained to me that I had used my anger, which is one of the stages in the grieving process, to fuel my recovery, because I knew beyond a shadow of a doubt that what I was saying was the truth. This anger could have taken on a destructive tone, but instead it forced me to not be a victim of those others trying to control my life in ways that I didn't want. I stood up to them by asking the obvious questions that would get me the results I wanted. I also became very aware that I was going to have to be in full control of my destiny, my life, and my finances; I had better learn quickly how to manage all the trusts that Terry's will had set up. It was finally going to be just what Jill wanted. I put myself at the top of the list for really the first time in my life..

One of the first things I did was to take my name off of the trusts set up for Terry's sons so that I no longer had to approve their requests (written to be the case until they turned forty). I did not want our relationship to be one where they had to be nice to me because they wanted some money. In our blended family, when it came to anything to do with his sons, it was Terry's decision alone—and rightly so, I thought; I wasn't their mother. Now that I was in charge, I saw things a lot differently. I sat the boys down in October of 2006 and explained to them that I saw no reason for them to have to go through me to get to their own money; they may as well start to learn how to handle it themselves. They agreed completely, and I'm sure this gesture went along way in earning their trust. I let them know I trusted them to handle their bequests; even if they didn't exactly know what to do, they knew enough to ask all the right people. This was a huge burden off my shoulders. I knew I didn't like the fact that I was controlled by a trust, so I reasoned, why would they like it?

The other major thing I did was to simplify Terry's various companies. Years before, high-paid lawyers and tax accountants had set up an elaborate system to avoid or delay paying taxes—legally, of course. Such things are common in the business world, but I saw it as a complicated web that contradicted the ease and simplicity with which I wanted now to live my life. I know this goes counter to what many successful business people would say, but I might say that some (not all) let the money control their lives, rather than letting it set them free to enjoy their lives. I wanted none of this game. "Simplify" became my mantra.

I also became keenly aware that money is power, especially in the business world, but less so in the spiritual world; which is where I was headed. I still had my business sense in me, but I was now very much aware that if I didn't use this money, this power, effectively it could destroy me. Money is like energy: if it flows easily and effortlessly, it provides fuel, but if it stagnates or used carelessly, its power can destroy.

It might seem to people who don't have a lot of money that it's exactly what they need to make them happy. In fact, it's the *love* of money, not simply *having* money, which can destroy you. However, everyone has the same neurosis about it if they don't have a good understanding of this truth. Balance is always the key to having a healthy relationship with money. I've had both situations in my life; money and no money; and I'm just learning to find the balance between the two.

So for me, it was easy to let go and not be in control of the trusts for the boys. It would be a while before I saw the other side of the same coin: I was also going to have to give up the need to control money in future relationships with a potential spouse, especially if he had less money than I did.

I learned many lessons about money: I prefer having it than not, I deserve it, I know how to handle it, and I can let it flow into areas that are of interest to me. This was the spiritual direction that I wished to manifest in my life. I initially felt compelled to do something good with all the money I now controlled. However, as I listened more during my meditations, I accepted that it would be okay if something didn't inspire me for several years. I didn't have to feel guilty about my abundance, nor did I have to feel compelled to spend it or use it to buy love or friendships. Money did not represent me, nor could it buy my happiness or health. My dad's limiting belief was that the only friend you have is the dime in your pocket. I didn't share that same belief. True friends and true love cannot be bought; like trust and respect, they have to be earned.

Fortunately for me, during all my legal and insurance hassles, I was able to make all my ends meet. It helped that John Pike, a good friend of ours, stepped up and took care of many things, not the least of which was to sell Terry's store. John had been the one who encouraged Terry to buy a franchise back when Terry was still searching for an opportunity to be his own boss. To get Terry's store ready to be sold immediately following the accident, John left retirement in Florida and hurried back north. All of our accounts had been frozen after the accident, and the trust officer was administering all of my financial affairs. Luckily, I trusted John to look after all those details.

I couldn't help but wonder about other people who had lost their spouses suddenly. How did they handle their mortgages or take care of their children if they didn't have any access to any funds? This is an important lesson, mostly for women (this is not to exclude men, but it's more true for women) who rely on their spouses. I can't stress enough that one should have one's own account in one's own name and perhaps even a separate line of credit. At the time of a tragedy, one really doesn't want to have to worry about money or cash flow.

I counted my blessings many times a day for the simple fact that Terry was a very good financial planner and that he included me in everything when it came to our financial affairs. According to statistics, money is the number one cause of all divorces and discord in families. After my experience dealing with Terry's estate, I learned one thing for sure: I needed to be in charge of my own affairs.

Chapter Eighteen—Back Home to My New Reality

As time went by, I experienced significant turning points in my recovery. By June of 2006, six months after the crash, I was finally able to drive myself around. Most of the apparatuses were off my legs and arms, and while my reaction time was slow, I could still manage to drive. I still used a cane for stability. Ironically enough, while I could drive myself somewhere, I didn't have enough stamina to do anything once I arrived. So often, just to get out of bed and the house, I would drive to a store, park out front, perhaps venture to the front doors—and quickly realize I was exhausted. Shopping or the thought of shopping might have been a diversion, but it actually held no interest for me whatsoever.

I spent a lot of time watching movies and TV. My head injuries precluded me from being able to concentrate on anything like writing or reading yet. It would take another year before I could start to write things down. In the meantime, I was still consumed with handling the will, the insurance companies, the bills, the funeral, and my own daily requirements.

About the middle of May, my wonderful niece Meagan came to live with me. She was in University in Calgary, but chose to work a summer job in Edmonton. I was well enough to manage on my own for her eight-hour workday, but I'm so grateful that she was there for me in the evenings. I was used to being alone during the day while Terry worked, but would have found the evenings and weekends unbearable on my own.

Meagan would buy all the groceries, make all my meals, do my laundry, and lovingly sit with me every night as we watched TV, played card games, or simply talked. Every night, we'd each pull an Angel card and share our destinies or lessons as outlined by the card we chose. I treasured every single moment we had together. She is a very loving soul and very mature for her age.

In mid-July one day, I was standing in the kitchen, leaning against the counter for support, and I suddenly exclaimed, "Oh my God, I can feel my feet!"

You might think I would have noticed earlier, but I didn't even know that I wasn't feeling them until I did! They were burned and sore and not very stable. As I was learning to walk, my left foot gave me a lot of pain, and it appeared my entire left arch had fallen, thus forcing me to pronate on that foot and walk on the edges. Oddly, it wasn't until October of 2007 that I insisted on seeing the foot specialist in Vancouver. He took one look at my left foot and clearly saw that it had been broken, most likely in the plane crash.

I don't know why I feel like defending the doctors who had initially worked on me immediately after the crash, but they really had so many other injuries on me to worry about—and since I couldn't walk until months later—they couldn't have been aware of the problem. My foot had simply been overlooked during my early treatment.

I gathered up my courage once again and agreed to another surgery. I'd have to go to Vancouver, and by then I had decided that I would move to Kelowna to begin my new life. The recovery, involving three months of not bearing any weight on my foot, would occur in Kelowna, where I would be alone. I had no team of angels. I had to cope on my own.

I knew beyond a shadow of a doubt that while it may have seemed crazy to leave my support team, I needed to keep moving toward the new life that I dreamed about. From my many unsettling experiences as a youth, I had grown into the type of person who does not stick their toe into the shallow end of the pool; I learned to jump into the deep end and figure out how to survive once I'm in it. So I jumped!

Perfect Princess Life...

"What lies behind us and what lies before us are tiny matters compared to what lies within us."

—Ralph Waldo Emerson

149

Part Four: My Spiritual Transformation Begins

Chapter Nineteen—Limiting Beliefs

Our karmic body carries our history of unresolved conflicts we have experienced in the past. These are built into our personality and self-image. It is the source of our reactions to every situation and every relationship we face from moment to moment. Our unconscious agitated emotions and feelings remain dormant in the form of discontent and a sense of "I'm not okay." This sense of insecurity resurfaces and gets reflected in the form of an emotional reaction to whatever is "triggering" you at any given moment. 85% of all health problems are caused by stress. When you remove the "cause," all the symptoms you experience as "effects" begin to heal and disappear. Stress is violence against your self. I am the predator and the prey. Under stress we see problems, not solutions.

—Yogi Amrit Desai

The excavation process was and is an integral part of my spiritual journey. Sometimes I refer to the process like peeling back the layers of an onion. Either way, once I started digging and looking at my childhood and all that went on in my life up until the accident, all the dramas and the traumas seemed to have a common thread. That thread was me! That might sound simple and obvious, but in reality, the stress that I created in my body, both prior to the accident and later through the hospital and legal dramas, was the first half of the equation, and a direct result of my victim like behaviors. According to Yogi Amrit Desai, "When emotional discontent shows up in the body, and the stressor remains unresolved, it often shows up in the form firstly as 'discomfort,' and then eventually some sort of 'disease'."

The second half of the equation was discovering I always had a choice. Just to be clear, I am not saying that I attracted the accident or that I *consciously* chose for it to happen.

Now however, in my quest to connect to my soul, which represents the inner source of wisdom and the divine right to happiness, I could see that some of these old behaviors, resulting from my subconscious limiting beliefs did not serve me anymore. The accident acted as a catalyst to allow me to see my truth and to take responsibility for my life. In the beginning I thought of it as a tragedy and I had to blame either myself or someone else for causing it. Later, as the truth was revealed to me one step at a time, I was able to see that every event in our lives is a gift from God.

All of these new thoughts were revealed to me only once I got connected to my own source. Through meditation, I finally listened to what my soul needed to tell me about the purpose of this accident-cum-gift. God continued to put in my path all the necessary people and events to push all my hot buttons or to keep me expanding into my fullest expression of my true self.

According to Esther and Jerry Hicks, authors of *The Vortex* and *The Law of Attraction*, "It is important that you acknowledge that you are a Vibrational Being, emanating Vibrational signals of desire. From your human form, you offer a vibration of what you want—because you know what you don't want, so you know what you do want—you cannot contemplate any subject without equal components of wanted and unwanted appearing vibrationally in your experience."

There was no doubt I had a lot of broken bones and badly injured tissues and muscles, but once that all healed, my emotional body needed the most work. It was my emotional needs and desires that were the most stunted throughout my life. Only once I perceived the accident as a gift did my body start to function with more ease. My mind settled down, so that I could finally sleep through the night with no drugs. When my anger at and frustration with all the lawyers and companies and people we were suing diminished, my bowel irritability improved. Once I let go of carrying the weight of the world on my shoulders (I initially felt 100 percent responsible for the legacy that Terry left me, including his son's trusts) and the host of responsibilities I had with all my material stuff, my neck, back, and shoulders stopped aching.

In everyday situations, I learned not only to honor what I was feeling, but also to express it more honestly. I started to ask for what served me the most. I didn't always give in automatically and accept the thought that others must know better, which had always left me feeling I was the one doing the accommodating. This included Terry's point of view (even though he had passed, I still found myself thinking what would Terry say), as well as my family and friends. I certainly did not want to be controlled by their potentially limiting beliefs along with my own.

Around year three to four of my recovery, I coincidentally met a very unique healer named Beverly Lenz, whose own personal midlife crisis led her to use her God-given gift of healing to help others. The method is called Belief Change Systems, or BCS. Using a combination of science and methods that access inner wisdom, BCS transforms cellular memory to release beliefs and traumas stored in your body at a cellular level. The BCS process utilizes muscle testing to communicate with the subconscious mind. All of my childhood beliefs were examined. Some beliefs are taught, and others are carried on a cellular level—you are born with them. Often they come from both sets of parents, but not necessarily so.

This process, this journey that I was now on, appeared in subtle ways, that in my previous "unconscious" existence I would have ignored. But now that I was shaken into a more alert consciousness, I could not help but marvel at all the ways, all the signs that the universe was trying to show me. God was simply showing me the way in no uncertain terms. I call it my crash Course to unconditional love and forgiveness.

The sub-conscious limiting beliefs that were hindering my true happiness and success in my life were:

> ➢ I have to be perfect to be loved

> ➢ Speaking my truth just makes matters worse

> ➢ All females in my family get fat

> ➢ Playing small makes me more likeable

> ➢ Don't question men in authority, for they know best. Females are "less than" males

> ➢ I am not worthy of love, trust, money, happiness or forgiveness

> ➢ My female sexuality is not to be honored or owned

- ➢ I am not capable of taking care of myself

- ➢ I have to look outside myself for happiness

Chapter Twenty—Feathers, Coins, and Other Messages From Above

About six months after the accident, I visited a medium that I had seen with Terry when I had convinced him to go with me about a year prior to the accident. It would be fair to say that Terry was not keen on this sort of thing, which he would refer to as hocus-pocus. However, that day this medium described one of the spirits in the room as having unusually large hands. She said the spirit, a relative of Terry's (Terry's dad) was saying 'Enjoy your life, work and worry less, love more.' What made Terry into a quasi-believer was the fact that his father, who had passed by then, did have unusually large hands *for* a man of his slight size. For an engineer to go beyond and actually believe ... well, that would have asked Terry to move very far outside his comfort zone. He had to see it to believe it, instead of believing it to see it! I could tell that this reading definitely peaked his curiosity, but still he wouldn't really let on that it could possibly be true.

I now wanted some answers to a number of questions. Was there any unfinished business we might have had together? What did Terry think now? What was he doing on the other side? Was he okay? Why did he have to go and not me? I wanted to connect with him one more time.

His sense of humor shone through that day, because the medium told me she saw Terry pointing to the top of his head and laughing. Just months before the accident, I had convinced him to take some herbs that promised to grow hair back on his bald spot. I gathered that on the other side, one could take on the image of any age. He now had his full head of hair back, and he wanted me to know this.

He also said he was sending his love, and that he was constantly with me by sending messages through the use of loose coins, feathers, and—the *pièce de resistance,* he was interfering with the electricity in our house. Ever since I returned from the hospital, all of the lights and some of the table lamps would inexplicably start to flicker, almost constantly. At first I had been worried and anxious about it, even asking a friend to change the electrical box, but after hearing this news I started to feel some comfort in knowing that Terry was just trying to communicate in a way that I might recognize. He knew I was electronically challenged and thus this would be our joke.

For quite some time now, I would find loose coins in front of me everywhere I went. I was doing a lot of looking down mind you, mostly because I was so unsteady on me feet. I also would find feathers in very odd places. When I was at Glenrose Hospital, I had a friend stay at the house. She later told me that one night a white feather floated back and forth in front of her as she was preparing a meal. I had not told her of my visit to the medium. I simply smiled and silently thanked Terry for watching over us!

One final message through the medium sent shivers through me. She told me Terry was sorry he had left me with the legal mess, and suggested I change lawyers. I had not mentioned anything about the case during our session, but she told me that Terry was aware of all that had been going on since he died. He also thanked me for the lovely service and the soapstone sculpture, which I had commissioned by a favorite artist of Terry's to house his ashes. I called it *Watching Over You.* He knew! My heart was pacified by all the validation I had received. As this was fairly soon after the accident and early in my recovery, I needed any sort of connection I could possibly get. I was grateful for all that was said during those visits.

She also mentioned that upon crossing over, Terry went into a frenzy on the other side, because he knew that I was going to be left with quite a few injuries and so he was frantically calling on all spirit guides to help the rescue team on Earth get to us in time. Obviously something was working, because it truly was a miracle that we were rescued at all.

A few other odd things happened that I realized were Terry's doing. One night, as Lois and I were lying in bed, about to start our evening ritual of her massaging my feet, she suddenly felt very sick to her stomach, and her chest started to tighten up. All of a sudden, we heard a loud "Pop!" The box carrying Terry's ashes was inside the nightstand and it literally expanded and made a loud popping sound. We didn't touch it at all; it did this all by itself.

Another unusual, but coincidental event occurred. One day in June, Kevin and his girlfriend at the time, were helping me de-clutter my house by putting on a garage sale of all the stuff I had to get rid of. In our back yard, nestled among several of our evergreen trees, sat a single white-tailed deer all afternoon. This deer wandered in around noon and didn't leave until around four—*exactly the length of time* of the garage sale!

The whitetail deer was Terry's favorite animal. I had decided to sell Terry's favorite painting of a while-tail deer to one of his hunting friends who had helped me place our two beloved Springer Spaniels in with another family after it became obvious I wouldn't be capable of caring for them. Giving away my babies, my animals, was another very painful experience, but I was numb to all my pain at the time. Plus, I knew I had to do what was right for them. I couldn't possibly care for them properly and I knew they deserved a loving family.

It was as if Terry was watching over and approving the sale. I watched as Kevin more than once curiously observed the deer and wondered aloud if it could be his dad. I knew in my heart of hearts Terry was peacefully approving of all that was going on.

> Deer has entered your life to help you walk the path of love with full consciousness and awareness, to know that love sometimes requires caring and protection, not only in how we love others, but also in how we love ourselves. When we move through life in the spirit of love for all beings, we can melt the barriers that separate us from others.
>
> - Google – Animal Spirit Guides
> and their meaning

Chapter Twenty-One—Inside The Vortex

Exactly one week before the first anniversary of the plane crash, I had my first ever out-of-body experience. It was a Monday morning, very early, and I was lying in my bed, drifting in and out of a light sleep. I became suddenly aware that I was outside of my body. I felt this very powerful vortex and heard a whooshing noise as I hovered over my body on the bed beneath me. Then I heard a tinkling like icicles in the dead of winter.

Suddenly the head and shoulders of a man appeared before me. I could see him quite clearly. He was kissing my abdomen reverentially; my first thought was that it must be Terry since I recognized a familiar bald spot on his head. I could hear voices saying that it was going to be okay, that I had the will to make a complete recovery. He was kissing me on my solar plexus, or my third chakra, which I knew was the chakra responsible for will and transformation.

Next I noticed that I was basking in a glorious feeling of unconditional love. I could also sense there were no time or space limitations. I moved my hands to caress the man's head lovingly and express my own gratitude to him, but as I did, the loud vortex returned, and just as forcefully as this energy appeared, it disappeared. I immediately fell back into my body.

By now, I was clearly awake. *What the heck just happened?* I thought. The force of the entry and departure had caused me to rock in my bed. By now my arms and legs were stretched out, searching for the edges of the bed. *Did I just imagine that, or was it for real?*

This experience was just as real as the imposition of those stranger's eyes looking at me from Terry's face just minutes before the plane crashed; just like that experience, this one was also something I couldn't deny. I saw the eyes then, and now I felt, heard, and saw this energy. I can't say for sure that the man kissing my abdomen was Terry, or an angel, or a spirit guide. Call him what you want, but I do know for certain that *someone* or at least some *energy* came to visit me that day.

The vortex brought the sound of energy from another world. The unconditional love was so beautiful that words could never convey it, but I know for sure that unconditional love is what I needed to learn. As I lay there reflecting over what just happened, I couldn't help but smile from ear to ear. I knew I was going to be okay and I was open to whatever was going to happen next … so … bring it on!

My next out-of-body experience occurred a couple of months later, again on a Monday morning. This time the exit from my body was less forceful and there was no sound. I spun like a top, not over and over, but rather around and around. The messages were again very clear: "Your life has been turned completely around and you need to see it from all angles and all sides."

With that thought, I was brought back down into my body. Then an electrical bolt of energy zigzagged its way up and down my body, stopping at every one of my injury sites as if to give it a little extra burst of healing energy. As it zipped around, I heard the message, "You will be completely healed; love yourself exactly as you are!"

Similar experiences continued for the next three or four months. Were they caused by my deep meditation? Were they simply messages from my spirit guides to assure me that I was going to be ok? I finally reached the following explanation: I was now on, or in, a different vibrational level. I had no fear of anything that was happening. In fact, I eagerly anticipated whatever would come next. I can't say if these amazing messages came from Terry wanting to help me, or if they were my own angels, or if they were simply God. All I know is that that sort of thing is possible. Certain multisensory people seem to have these gifts, while five-sensory people who do not quite often think you are basically nuts! Frankly, I don't blame them, until and unless it actually happens to you, it's a giant leap of faith to believe these things happen at all.

I continued to have more multisensory experiences, but they were not always as clear and not always about my injuries. Deepak Chopra describes this type of experience as "non-local." One such experience was very similar to the voice in the movie *Field of Dreams* that said, "If you build it, they will come." It sounded exactly like that voice, in that same sort of whisper.

These non-local experiences often centered on my paternal grandmother. She died when I was around ten or eleven years old. I usually heard a lot of whispering, repeated maybe three times before I could actually make out what was being said. Sometimes I would only actually hear the last word or two; it would sound like a voice whispering over and over, and then a word like "Wednesday."

While all this was happening, I was trying to sell my Edmonton house, so I interpreted it to mean that the following Wednesday the house would sell. In fact, my house did sell on a Wednesday, but three months later. At least my spiritual whisperer got the details correct!

These experiences were so real and so amazing to me. Humans are more than just our bodies; we are spiritual beings having a human experience. Our soul lives in eternity as a soul in another space-time continuum.

Chapter Twenty-Two—Learning To Meditate: An Inside Job

After my second back operation to remove the two metal rods in March 2007, I decided to learn to meditate. I was diagnosed with post-traumatic stress disorder (PTSD), so it was going to be a challenge to quiet my mind. But at least I could give it a try.

Not knowing anything more about meditating, two of my angel friends had taken a "primordial sound" meditation class earlier in the year, put on by the Deepak Chopra Centre. They'd raved about it. I had read a few of Chopra's books back in the late '90s; while certainly intrigued, I had never really investigated or thought more of delving into his teachings. Now, however, I simply thought this would give me something to do while I spent another six weeks recovering from my second back surgery.

Coincidentally, there was another weekend session coming up in Edmonton at the end of April, so Laurie and I decided it was time to enroll. They suggest that you practice meditating every day for twenty-one days in a row, starting slowly with ten minutes and eventually working up to thirty minutes, ideally twice a day. It wasn't like I had anything else to do; so much to my delight it gave me something different to look forward to every day.

At first, like any other novice, I found it difficult to quiet the mind. But with patience, I found I could reach the gap—the place between thoughts. It was in those gap times that my soul spoke to me!

I began by writing out in my mediation journal all that I wanted to attract into my life. At the top of my list was a spiritual partner, one who would already have an understanding of who God is and who just wanted to share the joy of living. Most importantly, I wanted a partner that put me first (next to God) in his life. I no longer wanted to apologize for my position in life. I wanted to sing, dance, and be happy.

My old list of criteria for a suitable partner simply did not ring true for me anymore. My partner didn't have to be powerful, tall, rich, or anything else for that matter. Instead, this time around, I really wanted a man who was already on his own spiritual journey. I knew now that everyone has baggage, and I was no exception.

I had three categories of desires: material, emotional, and spiritual. I would simply read my intentions before I started to meditate, and eventually, in the silent recesses of my mind, I would see and feel my soul talking to me and providing answers to my questions.

It is with great reverence and humbleness that my meditations had revealed to me the parts of my life that were so disconnected and incongruent with what I wanted to attract now. I would come face to face with these ugly parts of my personality when I finally looked in the mirror and saw the truth. These parts are known as our shadow selves. According to Debbie Ford, author of *The Shadow Effect* and *The Dark Side of the Light Chasers*, "We are masters of disguise, fooling others but also fooling ourselves. It's the lies we tell ourselves that we need to decipher. It is when we're not completely satisfied, happy, healthy, or fulfilling our dreams, we know these lies are in our way. This is how we recognize our shadows at work. "

The three qualities that we like the most in others, and the three qualities that we dislike the most in our enemies, are all parts of our personalities. Usually we only like to show the world our good parts.

I was no exception; I had long worn a mask that I thought cleverly hid the parts I didn't want the world to see. Now I could see I was simply looking in the mirror and seeing my reflection of that other person in myself.

In fact, the old adage to keep your friends close and your enemies closer actually started to make sense to me. I usually just tried to avoid people or situations I didn't like. Now, I was open to seeing that the reflected bad parts of me that were the cause of so much of my discomfort were just parts of my personality that I didn't want to admit to or own.

The Chopra Centre promotes an Ayurvedic approach to wellness, which means, very simply and briefly, that through proper nutrition, daily exercise, and meditation practice, one can achieve a state of balance in mind, body, and soul. This was part of my definition of success. I chose the Chopra Centre programs to guide me to this balance because I was impressed with their stories.

While both co-founders, Dr. Deepak Chopra and Dr. David Simon, are trained doctors in Western medicine, they both wanted to integrate Ayurveda with western medicine in a wellness clinic. The Chopra Centre is that extension of a life-long desire to teach body and mind awareness to everyone … at least those interested and searching for wellness, physically, mentally, and spiritually.

It was a real dream come true for me to be tutored and pampered by the Chopra Centre staff and the spiritual programs that gently exposed me to myself. Each day included morning yoga, a half-hour meditation, a ninety-minute glorious massage, and a bhasti (oil enema). The oil enema includes nourishing herbs and oils that are prescribed based on what your *dosha* is and whether or not you are in or out of balance. It helped eliminate toxins, whether they are environmental, physical, or emotional in nature.

I felt I was near the end of needing Western doctors, even though they had fixed my many broken bones. I had had enough of prescription drugs and surgeries. Now my real requirements were emotional and spiritual; I was ready to heal emotionally and the Chopra Centre treatments were centered on this part of my story and my healing

In my former perfect princess world, I would simply wave my magic wand and map out the perfect mate and life. He certainly couldn't be a workaholic—nor could he have any other addiction. While North American society in general turns a blind eye to workaholics, I would no longer stand the emotional toll it takes on families.

In the world of big business, work addition is not only acceptable behavior; it is often revered. Yet ask the partners who live with this type of addiction and they will tell you it is just as damaging to a relationship as many so-called unacceptable addictions such as alcohol, gambling, drugs, or even sex.

In the West, success is usually described in relation to business success. We never pay too much attention to looking inside for the elusive happiness we all seek. Even by my own new definition of success, I knew that I had to see things differently and to surrender to the universe. My meditations were making things clearer and clearer to me.

Deepak would explain that everyone has an addiction of some sort. Once I finally admitted to myself that the personality traits that I thought were good were in fact addictions, and then could I see that I was no better or no worse than everyone else. I lived in my own false sense of superiority that really masked an inferior sense of self. Only when I was willing to see the underneath part, the layers upon layers if you will, that motivated me toward my own addictions and thus what and who I attracted into my life, could I finally make some progress on my spiritual journey. During those months that turned into years of excavation work, I recognized the shadow parts of myself:

1. Perfectionism is an addiction. I am a perfectionist. Being with a perfectionist is difficult at the best of times, because whatever you do is never going to be good enough or perfect enough.

2. Power struggle. I needed to control everything. On the negative side of things, my need to be right exceeds my desire for happiness. Dr. Phil says, "Do you want to be right, or do you want to be happy?"

3. Trust issues, particularly blaming others. I don't truly trust either others or myself easily. Trust is tantamount in any relationship. A partner needs to know you have their back and are not working against you in whatever situation comes up. Trust also takes faith.

4. Judgment. I judge others and determine inferiority or superiority far too quickly. My back up is to be superior to others: I am more worthy than you. This is simply a mask that covers a lack of self worth.

5. Workaholic. I can never do enough; I always had to prove to others and to myself that I was worthy, by performing and churning out unbelievable amounts of work. I did it at the expense of my relationships, my health and my true happiness.

6. Avoids pain/confrontation. I'm numb to my real feelings and therefore cannot even tell the truth of how I'm feeling to myself nor to anyone else that I am in a close personal relationship with. Honest communication, speaking up and telling my truth has been a challenge for me in all areas of my life, both professionally and personally.

I would not have been willing or able to look at myself in the mirror and see my shadow self if it weren't for the accident. For this I am grateful. Yes, the perfect princess has a shadow self! I'm not even embarrassed to admit any of these personality traits. In fact, it is humbling and yet very freeing. I can still love and be loved exactly as I am now. Equally important, I can love someone else who has similar or different shadows. Now I see perfection in my imperfections! The even bigger picture of the true story was still yet to unfold.

Louise L. Hay, internationally renowned author and lecturer, explains in her book *You Can Heal Your Life,* that the limiting beliefs and ideas are often the cause of illness and you must be willing to do the mental work to heal almost anything.

The following lists my physical problems as a result of the accident. I had to look at all these areas one by one and acknowledge the truth in each one of the probable causes and then diligently create a new thought pattern in order to heal myself. I learned to do this once I learned to meditate.

Problem	Probable Cause	New Thought Pattern
Accidents	Inability to speak up for the self, rebellion against authority, belief in violence.	I release the patterns in me that created this. I am at peace. I am worthwhile.
Ankles	Inflexibility and guilt. Ankles represent the ability to receive pleasure.	I deserve to rejoice in life. I accept all the pleasure life has to offer.
Back	Represents the support of life.	I know that life always supports me.
(Middle)	Guilt. Stuck in all that stuff back there. "Get off my back."	I release the past. I am free to move forward with love in my heart.
Bone Problems		
Breaks/ Fractures	Rebelling against authority	In my world I am my own authority, for I am the only one who thinks in my mind.
Bowels	Fear of letting go of the old and no longer needed.	Letting go is easy.
Constipation	Refusing to release old ideas. Stuck in the past. Sometimes stinginess.	As I release the past, the new and fresh and vital enter. I allow life to flow through me.

Problem	Probable Cause	New Thought Pattern
Burns	Anger. Burning up. Incensed.	I create only peace and harmony within myself and in my environment. I deserve to feel good.
Foot Problems	Fear of the future and of not stepping forward in life.	I move forward in life with joy and with ease.
Injuries	Anger at the self, feeling guilty.	I now release anger in positive ways. I love and appreciate myself.
Joints	Represent changes in direction in life and the ease of these movements	I easily flow with change. my life is Divinely guided. I am always going in the best direction.
Knee Problems	Stubborn ego and pride Inability to bend. Fear. Inflexibility. Won't give in.	I am flexible and flowing forgiveness, understanding, compassion. I bend and flow with ease and all is well.
Muscles	Resistance to new experiences. Muscles represent our ability to move in life.	I experience life as a joyous dance.
Neck Problems	Refusing to see other sides of a question. Stubbornness, Inflexibility.	It is with flexibility and ease that I see all sides of an issue. There are endless ways of doing things and seeing things, I am safe. All is well in my heart now.
Pain	Guilt. Guilt always seeks Punishment.	I lovingly release the past. They are free and I am free.
Wrist	Represents movement and ease.	I handle all my experiences with wisdom, with love and with ease.

Chapter Twenty-Three—An Empty Canvas for My Emotional Healing to Begin

As a means to fill some of my very long and lonely days, I started journaling. It was cathartic for me. I made my first journal entry at the end of June 2007; it took me a year and a half to even be comfortable enough to actually sit and start writing. I poured my thoughts and feelings onto the lined pages of a pink leather journal that a good friend had given me for my forty-eighth birthday. Even if I couldn't identify what I was really feeling, I just wrote and wrote almost every day and for several months. I knew eventually it would come together.

I started the old-fashioned way, writing it out longhand. My pace was extremely slow and my writing was illegible at times, but my feelings were raw and real. Sometimes there were nine months between entries, but still I persevered. Journaling helped by not only keeping an accurate accounting of people, places, and things, but it also gave me a different perspective to ponder over as the years of recovery went by. Being on Percocet for so long definitely affected my brain function. I could recall the past, as in before the accident, but the present details were blurry at best unless I wrote them down just as or after they happened.

On one hand, I felt cocooned in love. On the other hand, as I started to put the pieces of my shattered life back together, my thoughts filled with fear. What could I change about these fears if I wanted to grow spiritually? I was battling my thoughts and my feelings. Perhaps we are all in this battle all the time: my ego mind was trying to control the shots, but my new connection to my heart was speaking more loudly, and I knew my soul was sending messages as well. It was beginning a necessary journey. Admittedly, I was still thinking and not really trusting my feelings about a lot of things, but when I meditated, I felt I was connecting with what my soul was trying to tell me. Trusting it did take a while, but soon, I couldn't deny the truth anymore. I started to surrender for real.

As I peeled away the layers of some very deep-seated emotions like anger, resentment, and disappointment, I discovered that many of my beliefs that were valid and true for me before the accident were now on the table for questioning. I very much felt the "disconnect" between my old thoughts and my new feelings. When I paused to figure out where in my body this disconnect lived, I started to connect more dots. I felt like I had been catapulted forward spiritually: God wasn't nudging me gently anymore but was hitting me over the head with a two-by-four. Fortunately, that forced time in bed to heal all my broken body parts was exactly what I needed to heal my soul as well. I needed to be still, to reflect, and most of all, to listen. All the answers to whatever questions I might have had before the accident, as well as the reason for this accident, were revealed to me almost from the moment I awoke to find Terry dead and myself alive

But what was I going to do with the answers? To be sure, I'm not saying I know all the answers now—I'm not even sure I know all the questions! My response is still my choice to make, and one that I will make every day on this new spiritual path. God will love me either way!

For a good eighteen months immediately following the accident,

I existed in an altered state of consciousness—inside the vortex, one might say—and this vortex was filled with nothing but loving thoughts from everyone and everything around me. I can joke that it was the drugs, but I honestly believe that this new and unfamiliar state was my second chance, a gift from God. All I had to do was surrender and trust. If I could do that, unconditional love would flourish. Peace could happen. My body would heal and function optimally if I let go of the points of view that caused all my discomfort in the first place.

From a micro-perspective, love is the answer to each person's problems; from a macro-perspective, love is the answer to the world's problems. Sadly, the planet will not change until and unless we collectively alter our consciousness to believe in more love, more compassion, and more tolerance. Do I need to say it? *Not* more war, *not* more separateness, *and not* more hatred for those that are different from us. We are all connected, and what we do to another, we really do to ourselves. Look around, it is everywhere on this planet and with the social media and Internet; it is instantly obvious to everyone... if we stop denying it in ourselves.

In fact, many truly great spiritual leaders and teachers have been teaching these very same spiritual truths for centuries. I feel awkward even comparing myself to a spiritual teacher, but in fact, I just happened to be given the unique opportunity of teaching it through my writings. I was humbly given a peek into how different this human experience on Earth could be like if we just believed, had faith, and loved unconditionally.

Marianne Williamson, a present day spiritual teacher and author of many books including *A Return to Love: Reflections on the Principles of a Course in Miracles* talks about fearing our greatness. It is not our smallness that really holds us back. I know now one of my greatest fears is one of greatness. All along I thought my fear was that I wasn't good enough so I had to play small. There is nothing enlightened about playing small so that others around you won't feel insecure.

Now I was going to have to take a step toward my greatness, toward my real purpose for having survived this tragedy.

I initially resisted writing my story, partially because all my friends kept saying I should write a book. Even though I knew deep down that I would, I had to wait until it could be real and truthful. "Should" didn't motivate me. I had to remember that I wanted to do this as inspiration to any and all who may experience a similar tragedy someday. There is light … there is a reason. I had to write only from my experience and let some other learned spiritual guru explain exactly what was occurring. However, once the two lined up for me, I felt more comfortable telling my unbelievable survival story, my truth … now with all masks off.

Still, at first, writing exhausted me after very little effort. My stamina would come around, but not for many years. However long it took, it was just going to have to be. Being real seemed extremely vulnerable, uncomfortable, and unfamiliar to me. However, the divine two-by-four to the head had knocked some sense into me. I was going to have to do the work and let go of the past in order to feel the freedom and thus internal peace, I had wanted so badly.

I was redefining myself moment by moment. I had an empty canvas to begin with and the truth was, with my abundance at hand, I could paint whatever picture I wanted. What would I choose with my knowledge directing me? What did I want, truly? How willing would I be to go for what I really wanted? Could I trust myself enough to differentiate between what I really wanted or would I choose based on what other people thought I should do? More importantly, would I choose my future based on fear like I had done so far all my life? All possibilities were open to me; all I had to do was trust myself and choose with an open heart.

My fears had nothing to do with crashing in an airplane, but rather a much bigger picture that involved a lot of my own limiting beliefs about everything: men, money, position, power, trust, and of course, my own self-worth.

I was still transitioning from being empowered by outside things to being empowered by my inner truths. Gary Zukav, author of *The Heart of the Soul,* would describe this as being authentically empowered. As I started to venture out on my own, God put squarely in my path the exact set of circumstances I needed to experience in order for me to realize why I was meant to live instead of leave this world. I later learned that this truth is based on a vibrational match, according to *The Laws of Attraction.* Be careful what you ask for in your prayers ... you just might get it!

Until now, I had always thought it was something outside of me that would make me happy—the relationships I was in, the places I'd been, the clothes I wore, or even the titles I might have had. Happiness was never about looking inside, or to a connection with a higher power. I was always the one in control. I always thought if it was meant to be, it was up to me to make it happen. I didn't really believe God even played a minor role in this picture, let alone that she was in charge!

I want you to know that I didn't have to conclude any of this as a result of this crash. I simply could have gone on living my new life with all the same old beliefs. Once I started on the spiritual path, it was very obvious that there was absolutely no use in continuing with this meaningless charade. My victim days were tiring, even to me. I was a warrior. This I knew for sure. Alas, what I discovered about me on the inside really wasn't so bad after all, but in fact, it was worth celebrating. I just needed to speak up and tell my truth.

I had cleverly lived behind a façade for forty-seven years. I finally had the courage to take off the many masks and just be open to whoever was underneath it. Anything to do with true or honest feelings was foreign to me but I was now willing to expose myself ... to find myself.

The first layer that I peeled back revealed that my true feelings were valid and were to be listened to. I had never learned that it was okay to feel whatever I felt. I was completely stifled as a young girl. My feelings were outwardly guarded, while inwardly they often ate me up. In fact, physical problems were starting to show up in my body again. The third chakra is the point in the body that deals with will and self-worth. I examined how I also willingly gave away my power, especially to men, including my dad, my first husband Ted, and most certainly to Terry. I was determined not to do this with my next relationship if I chose to have one at all. I needed to own what was rightfully mine and be ok with my power.

By all outward appearances, my friends and acquaintances would say I was quite confident. No one would have been able to see the inward discontent that my soul actually felt. How could they? I barely knew it.

For the time being, getting on with my life meant I had to deal with my new reality. Every minute of every day I was preoccupied with doing something aimed at healing. My overachieving nature grew subdued, I didn't have to prove anything to anybody; overachieving simply masked my own lack of self-worth.

Equally important to the physical healing were those spiritual messages I kept receiving. Often, as I lay in bed, I would remember the stranger's eyes transposed over Terry's eyes in the plane. I can't say they haunted me in an uncomfortable way, but I never forgot them. I had no idea whose eyes they were yet, nor why I was given this vision. Was it a gift from God? Was it some kind of message for which I would someday get an answer? I could only imagine as I lay there recovering.

Most of the balls Terry and I had had in the air had all dropped by now. My new, empowering choices concerned which I would let go completely, and which I would choose to pick up and start juggling again. Something had to change, so I started with where I was going to live. It was painful to be confined to a home where Terry and I had once shared so many happy memories. Now my house felt like a noose tightening around my neck, strangling any new thoughts and hope

I might have for my future. It was a constant reminder of what had been. I just couldn't cope physically or emotionally anymore with my house. Plus, I desperately wanted to simplify my life—and that meant downsizing big time. I started the simplification process by deciding to sell and move to Kelowna.

However, we had begun renovations on a house in BC we had bought in 2002, just weeks prior to the accident; in fact, it was gutted when the accident occurred. The whole time I was convalescing, this house renovation was underway in Kelowna. Fortunately, I had spent most of the previous year making all the design and decorating decisions. Since interior design was one of my gifts, even after the accident, it was still easy for me and still very exciting and kept my mind off of my pain. I had something to look forward to.

Originally, it was only going to take four to five months for the total renovations, which would have made it ready just after the service for Terry took place in May 2006. In a moment of synchronicity, an unfortunate water accident occurred about the same time, which precipitated a whole new round of insurance claims and more renovations that further delayed the readiness for now about another year. As a result of that, I thought maybe I could move to Kelowna after all.

Of course, in reality there was no way I could handle that now-renovated home either. It felt very much like I was holding onto a dream that had died with Terry, and I had to accept the fact that that house was not part of my new dream. I listed it with a realtor in August and had an offer within three days. But I didn't want to let the dream of living in Kelowna die ... not yet. In the meantime, I would go back to Edmonton and figure things out. Real estate in Edmonton was on fire. So if I sold that house too ... where, God, would I live?

Chapter Twenty-Four—As If God's Hands Were On Mine

Just before I left for Kelowna to check on the renovations in June 2007, I found myself being drawn to a spiritual website called Tut. com ("tut" stood for "Think Unbelievable Thoughts"). I had been receiving daily blessings—kind of like inspirational thoughts—for quite some time now, but didn't know there was a section on this website called the Village.

For whatever reason that day, I noticed the Village and clicked to discover that it was like a meeting place for spiritually like-minded souls to get to know one another. Because at that time I still had wanted to move to Kelowna, I decided to do a search for a spiritual friend in that area. Lo and behold, once I found how to search for potential friends, I set my criteria and pushed send!

The program asked me to create my own profile. I started to read through the personal questions, which would normally have turned me off immediately. This time, although it took me a good forty-five minutes, I persevered. At first I found myself thinking, *I used to be* and *I used to do*, but it soon became clear that I was not really sure how to describe myself anymore. I know I was doing a lot of self-exploration, but thinking about it and putting it down on paper was

179

quite a bit different. So as if God's hands were on mine, I just started typing from my heart. I didn't lead with my plane crash story, of course, but I said what I wanted to attract now into my life, along the lines of the desires I outlined in my meditation journal.

After maybe two hundred words at best, I submitted the form, closed my computer, and forgot about it. It wasn't until I returned from my ten-day visit to Kelowna, at the end of June, that I realized that I had sent a wink to somebody who looked interesting. So some twenty days later, I thought I would check ... and sure enough, my wink had elicited a response from someone from Vernon, some thirty minutes from Kelowna. I was attracted to his screen name: Brave Heart.

He said he liked to cook Italian; he liked to play golf; and from his picture, I could tell he liked to work out. He also described himself as spiritual, not religious. The last place you'd catch him was in a bar, and the last job he would ever take would be as a politician. He also checked that he was self-employed and had an average income. His favorite author was Edgar Case. He said he was forty years old and divorced. I thought that was a little young, but I had put my criteria of ages to be between forty and fifty-five. And hey, I might like a younger man anyway.

> Love looks not with the eye but with the mind
> And therefore is winged Cupid painted blind.
> —William Shakespeare

Chapter Twenty-Five—Brave Heart: My Love Story

What's the fairy tale story about a princess kissing a frog and he turns into her prince? I'm not a real princess, but maybe I am playing out an archetype of some sort. After my new cyber friend, Brave Heart and I exchanged a few e-mails, I quickly suggested we talk and get to know one another the old-fashioned way: on the phone. I trusted that I could give him my phone number safely, and so started our hour-long phone conversations every day for a good month before we met for our much-talked-about first date, a picnic in the park.

He sent me a picture of himself and had clarified with me he was in fact fifty; he just hadn't bothered to go back in and change his mistake after he accidentally hit a four instead of a five. He was also new to the site. I teased I would send him a picture of me from high school at first, but it might take a while because I didn't know how to send pictures in a JPEG format.

In his picture he was wearing a baseball cap pulled down over his eyes, so I really couldn't see them. He was dressed in workout shorts and a muscle shirt, which clearly showed his very strong body. There was no doubt I was instantly attracted to his very fit body and what

I perceived his lifestyle habits to be. I also liked his description of his likes and dislikes.

A couple of weeks later, we were on the phone and I was telling him that I had just witnessed a baby robin fall out of its nest on my deck. I had approached it, and as I did, the little bird opened its beak really wide, anticipating that my presence must be its mother ready to offer some food. There was a short silence, and then Brave Heart said, "You know, my real name is Robin." He went by Rob, so I'd assumed it was short for "Robert"; Small coincidence... maybe?

After our conversation I went out to see what happened to the little chick ... miraculously, it had managed to fly away—there was no sign of the little robin either on the deck or in its nest.

One night as we were revealing our truths to each other, I remember feeling very compassionate towards what he described as his own "plane crash". He claimed that, and a few other less than proud moments in his life, had brought him to his knees as well. He found God in having to face his addiction to alcohol, but he overcame it all ... one day at a time. He had been sober for over six years. Wow: a humble man! He prayed for a partner that didn't drink.

We spent over an hour going through the twelve-step program; I was not familiar with the details, just that one existed. Over the phone, together, with his heart on his sleeve, he went through each step, and I just listened. I connected with his pain. He was on the right path again. Who was I to judge him for his past? I could only marvel at his courage, as he marveled at mine.

Just before we were to meet for our picnic in the park, Robin had sent me a picture of his face, and when I first looked into his eyes, I had this instant recognition: those were the eyes, *exactly* as I saw them in Terry's eyes minutes before we crashed! Could this be possible, and what could it mean?

I started to cry; instinctively I knew this meant something important, although I was still a little incredulous that such a thing could happen. Could it be Terry knew he would be passing and was sending me a message through his eyes, as one last attempt to show me his love? Or...was it my soul trying to let me know my future if I chose to survive this crash? Still, I didn't really know the answer as to what that experience actually meant.

I was trembling and tears came to my eyes. I hadn't thought about that experience for quite some time and certainly was careful about whom I told it to, but now could this be for real? I remember telling Robin about the whole "eye" thing; rather than freaking out, he believed every word and felt a very strong connection from our very first phone call. Yikes!

I now was inextricably drawn to meet this man in person. I kept vacillating back and forth with whether I was actually ready or not for another relationship. Did I even want a relationship? Did it have to even be a relationship? All I know is that, I kept my eyes wide open, as well as, my heart.

I spent the next two weeks with Robin. We did have our picnic in the park and that is where we fell in love—I finally had my prince. Only this time, all he had was his heart to give me ... and that's all I wanted. He was simply more spiritual than material. Exactly what I was looking for.

That beautiful bright sun-shiny day in the park, I literally got down on my hands and knees and rolled around in the grass for the first time in what felt like ages. I was so thankful for the grass, the trees, and the flowers, and for the simplicity of spending the afternoon together, Robin reading to me from *Conversations with God*. We were just simply being! Nothing fancy, just connecting to Mother Earth and to each other. We couldn't help ourselves.

We lounged and drank in the love that was flowing effortlessly back and forth between us. We were intoxicated most of the time ... but with love only. It wasn't even hard for me to trust Robin, as he was able to tenderly show me a way to let the good feelings of making love be okay... more than okay, even. It was natural and normal and it just felt right. I felt beautiful again, and very much connected to my body. I even have to admit that I never once thought about Terry or felt guilty, as if I was somehow betraying him by being with another man. I guess I was ready and willing to accept the fact that I had to move on and that Terry was never coming back.

In fact, on several occasions that week, it was like time stood still. My heart and third-eye chakras were absolutely beaming at me once again. We never noticed the time or the days, as one simply slipped into the other. One day, in midafternoon, I went to Rob's living room to listen to some music while he napped. I remember I was listening to John Legend's song "Make Room for my Love," when all of a sudden my iPod went dead. I got up off the couch and went into the kitchen. There it was: a three-inch white feather underneath the kitchen chair. The only thing missing was the flickering lights! But the iPod took their place; it had had power a few minutes before, but now inexplicably stopped working. I checked, and it wasn't that it was merely out of juice. Was Terry watching and giving me his approval? In my emotionally intoxicated state ... I believed he was.

By the time I went back to Edmonton, Robin had got down on bended knee and said with his hand over his heart, "Sweetheart, all I have is my heart to give you, if you will take it." I melted with love for the first time in my life.

Around this time, I was starting to understand that God had given me exactly what I asked for: a spiritual partner who wants to rejoice and love life with me. He did show me those eyes. Could it be anymore clear? Did God so lovingly show me these eyes, so that I might look in the mirror to see my true self, shadows and all, as well as, my future?

Robin – Robin Redbreast is the traditional herald of
spring for many. Its appearance and song is a sign of

new life returning. Spring is the time of new birth. This is the season, which brings a rhythm of emergence. Like the robin, now is the time to sing forth your own song if you truly wish new growth. A new spring is upon you and now is the time to stretch yourself. Extend yourself outwards into new areas of light. You will find your efforts successfully rewarded.

—Andrews, Ted, *Feathered Omens; Messenger Birds from the Spirit World,* Jackson, TN; Dragonhawk Publishing, 2009.

Chapter Twenty-Six—Synchronistic Events

In the meantime, I was inexplicably open to love and was now focused on each day with Robin. His voice and his manner turned me on, and I found myself very ready for whatever and wherever this journey would take me. I couldn't help but wonder if God was truly answering my prayers. The connection I felt both spiritually and physically was beyond what I thought possible. Our love seemed really intense and real. I couldn't help myself as I felt so much love and tenderness that I actually told Rob I loved him!

I felt I couldn't face the long, cold Edmonton winter either by myself or in my St. Albert house. I had not received any offers that summer, so I decided to take the Chopra Center's "SynchroDestiny" course in San Diego. Laurie, my life-long friend and angel, came with me.

The course was as exceptional as the "Seduction of Spirit" course I had taken earlier in the summer. I took away the knowledge that I simply had to take notice of the seemingly random events that occur—like when a friend calls and you were literally about to pick up the phone to call her. This isn't coincidence; it's universally inspired. It's synchronicity.

One evening during the class, we played this I-Ching game and we were advised to write down a question, or a situation, or a person, or something else that we were unsure of. As we followed a series of seemingly random questions, that included tossing of a quarter, "Unity" came as the answer.

Everywhere I turned that week, all points led me back to Robin. If I think back at the time, I know I was having doubts, because the ego mind is the cause of all problems. My heart was saying yes, but was in conflict with what my *old* ego side of my personality wanted in a partner. All my life I led with my brain, but this accident was helping me realize in order to be happy and find true peace and harmony I needed to lead with my heart.

When you are open to noticing the synchronistic events that occur on a daily basis and *really* be open to them, then you begin to see the dance of the universe, as Deepak would describe it as. The power comes in the choosing. No one choice is necessarily right or wrong; all options are available. Good luck is just taking advantage of an opportunity that you are already prepared for. I took a deep breath and plunged in to trusting the universe. Why not? Everything else worked for me when I cooperated with it.

I reminded myself that day, that while many things in my life as I knew it were over, it was still my dream to move to Kelowna. Now was the perfect opportunity. I decided to stop over in Kelowna on the way back. I checked out the Kelowna property that I had really liked some four months earlier, but mainly because my Edmonton home wasn't selling; I was a little unclear about putting an offer on yet another property. I wanted to simplify, not expand my real estate holdings!

As I was calling Sylvia, my Kelowna realtor, the very next day, she exclaimed, "I was just about to call you. The listing realtor for that property just called me to say the price has been reduced." Thinking that I had already seen the price reduction, I concurred, and she said, "No they've dropped the price again."

Now I was interested. I made an appointment to see it again. It just felt right. So, I made the offer that day, and within six hours I was the proud owner of a new condo!

Now I really had to sell the St. Albert properties (house and condo). As if the universe had conspired with me, I flew home on a Tuesday, and by the next day (remember Wednesday?) I had a reasonable offer. I accepted it and the rest is history.

Take the fork in the road, Jill!

Chapter Twenty-Seven—Exposing The Truth

I thought this foot surgery done in January 2008, would be my final surgery. In the end, however, I still had one more surgery in September 2008, two-and-a-half years after the plane crash; to remove the nine screws they had inserted to rebuild my collapsed arch in my left foot. Initially, it had been misdiagnosed and as time wore on and my pain continued, it became obvious I would have to have it fixed to be able to walk with some comfort and ease.

I wanted to rid my body of some of the toxins that I felt were accumulating because of all the drugs and anesthesia I had been pumping into it for the past two years. I decided to attend another Chopra Centre event titled "Perfect Health". This program; which included *panchakarma* (five actions) is a cleansing and rejuvenation program for the body, mind, and consciousness. It is known for its beneficial effects on overall health, wellness, and self-healing.

The lawsuit was in full swing by now. Two days of grueling examination for discovery in early spring of 2008 kept me focused on my recent foot surgery and even more determined to tell my truth and not feel like I had to apologize for any part of it. I told myself to remain calm, the truth will come out, and all those whom we were suing would be held accountable. Still, however, despite my intention of not worrying about the lawsuit, it continued to weigh heavily on my mind.

I was still having trouble sleeping, as I couldn't turn my mind off at night. I continued to have dreams, not really nightmares, but certainly scary. I would go over and over the scenes when I heard the rescuers say, "Two black and four red." I still wanted to scream at them, "You don't know who that is ... that's my husband. Check him again!" My PTSD coupled with my constant neck, back, shoulder, wrist and foot pain kept me in a never ending negative cycle.

Now the team of opposing lawyers insisted on knowing all the minute details regarding Terry's business dealings, our lifestyle, and my supposed injuries. Every small thing about our life was being scrutinized, and I felt harshly and unfairly judged for having a good life. This left me feeling defensive and, quite frankly, angry. It seemed that the emphasis was always on something other than the fact that my husband was dead and I and the other four survivors were left with a lot of serious injuries.

I felt like I had to give them the "right" answers. When I did, they weren't happy, because their intention in my case was to prove Terry wasn't as successful as it said on paper. I was telling my truth and not being heard! I didn't feel like my true feelings were being validated. Maybe not surprising to them, but certainly to me, the defendants were trying to make it like it was not their fault, that somehow we, the plaintiffs, caused this accident. I was not privy to the other plaintiffs' cases; occasionally, I talked with the two ladies from Toronto, but we were more focused on supporting each other through our numerous operations and next steps to recovery. We did not discuss our individual cases.

The most frustrating thing for me was that I had to visit so many doctors from both sides. They almost didn't accept that my foot problem was as a result of the plane crash! Eventually they did see it our way. Still, repeating the same story over and over again did not help me in trying to move on with my life. Keeping all the dates for these appointments was a challenge for me, because I still had memory problems and often got very confused. Plus, most of them were in Vancouver, which involved a lot of travel and staying in hotels, none of which was comfortable for me.

Obviously, I can't go into much detail about anything to do with regards to the outcome of the lawsuit. Suffice to say, the emotional and physical pain resulting from the litigation process was equally as burdensome as was the actual accident and loss of my husband.

On a positive note, an agreement was reached out of court and the case was finally settled on December 21, 2008, just shy of three years since the plane crash. It's still surprising to me that no one agreed to take responsibility for the actual engine failure, but that's the way our flawed system is set up. It's not designed for victims. Then again, I didn't want to be a victim to this or anything else. The toll on my emotional and physical body was not worth the settlement.

The findings and resulting report issued by the Transportation Safety Board (a body independent of Transport Canada) is a public document, but to my knowledge at the time of press for this book, little if any of their recommendations have been implemented. That would have been the only worthy thing to come from this, but as of yet, it has not changed any aviation laws in Canada. Sadly, unless and until things change, one can realistically expect similar accidents to happen. And they have. That's all I can say about that.

I will add that my team of lawyers was incredibly respectful of my family and our unique situation. I did feel that they were working toward the best solution under very bad circumstances. I can respect that they feel they are doing good and fulfilling a very valid purpose in coming to the aid of accident victims, for what is always a very bad situation. Their firm specializes in handling plane crashes. Another thing for which to be extremely grateful!

Chapter Twenty-Eight—Steady Pose, Full Breath, and Awareness

During the "Seduction of Spirit" course in Whistler I took just prior to meeting Robin, I was reintroduced to yoga. In reality, all I could do was chair yoga, as getting up and down off the floor was still a struggle for me. Still, I got re-inspired.

The teacher was so exceptional that I felt, even in my still-stiff state, I could do this! My former "perfect" self would never have been able to be okay with not doing the poses exactly right. However, in my new self, I was made aware that it doesn't matter what it looks like; it's the intention behind it that counts.

Slowly, very slowly, I was starting to feel less soft tissue pain. I can say I even felt supple. True to form, from a weeklong course that included some chair yoga, I decided to take a three-hundred-hour Beginner Yoga Teacher Training class. I still wanted to be challenged, but this time, I didn't need to perform for anybody but me ... because it was my choice.

Of course, how that all happened was synchronistic as well. Robin and I had gone down to Texas in April 2008. On the closing night I sat with a lady from Vancouver who happened to be a yoga teacher. She was telling me about a couple in Kelowna who had a yoga studio.

I was so new to Kelowna that I followed up immediately, went to a yoga class, and became hooked.

Harshad (his Sanskrit name; Western name Jeff) and his wife Sonya were Kripalu yoga devotees. Without too much more thought, I was going with the universe. I took their last spot! I wanted to connect to people of like mind in my new community. I was starting to like this "go with the flow" thinking, or what some call universally inspired events that always seem to happen at the right time.

I thought I could inspire other people who had suffered with similar injuries. I could show them that all you have to do is have the intention of lifting your arm over your head. With practice, you'll get there. Furthermore, you don't ever have to do a lotus position. Whew! That was a relief.

I enrolled in September 2008 and would graduate in May 2009 as a full-fledged beginner yoga instructor. However, in the end, I did it for myself. I really didn't have the desire to teach it, but I do continue to practice. I simply wanted to challenge myself, because I knew it would be good physically as well as spiritually. Little did I know that I would continue to ride the waves of life!

This intensive course delved not only into the history of yoga, but also into the philosophy. It was so rich in its content that I could never do it justice by trying to explain it, but suffice to say that yoga as the union of body and mind is practiced both on and off the mat. It was through my learning here that more dots got connected. I started to see my direction more clearly. I also started to rebuild the container for my life. I examined both what I had and what I really, really wanted. As the lawsuit was coming to an end and my body started to recover from the emotional trauma, I assessed what I wanted to put back into my container. What was working for me and what wasn't? The areas I explored were friends, family, purpose, and love.

Meditation had become a very effective tool for me: simply being quiet and listening to the universe and to myself enabled me to observe what wave I was riding at the moment. I learned not to judge what was going on, or what part of the wave I was on, but rather, I learned to sit on the shores of the ocean and observe with no judgment, no attachment to outcome ... just be. I let the feelings ride that wave. Fortunately, as my teachers liked to say, "This too shall pass." You ride one wave, it passes, and another one comes along.

I was connecting the dots, the traumas, and the dramas in my life to simply being a wave. The flow of life, as in the ebb and tide of the ocean just continues to happen. I can't stop it. I can, however, observe it ... and once again it's my choice as to how I react. It sounds simple, and it is, if you let it be so. It's definitely my path to more harmony and peace in my life. My body loved this connection!

One of the exercises involved revealing one of our biggest fears to the class—one that no one would know unless we told them. I remember saying that I feared that Robin was taking advantage of me and that I didn't trust our love and myself.

No sooner did I say those words aloud than I felt a lightning bolt hit me between the eyes. Did I have to experience another crash to get it? Was I going to continue to play the victim? So I simply thought what am I waiting for? All these courses, all these signs that I had been literally shown, were all adding up to one choice—love or fear. Love is love; fear is "false evidence appearing real."

I chose love! Pretty much that week, I made the decision to form a spiritual partnership with Robin. What was I waiting for? This relationship is what I wanted. So all my fears of what other people, including my family would think, and even what I would think, melted away as I took my power back and knew that the negative emotions that held me back—Rob not measuring up to my very high expectations of what a man should do, my lack of trust, being controlling, feeling resistance—all lived on the side of fear. The side of love included emotions like joy, harmony, peace, laughter, fun, and integrity. The choice was mine.

The trinity of yoga practice is steady pose, full breath, and awareness. I was beginning to integrate that philosophy into my life and it was working! Like the beginner yogini that I was, I felt like I was taking baby steps toward my new life of love, peace, and harmony.

Continuing on my quest to validate all the things that had happened to me, Robin and I decided to enroll in the Authentic Power Program week at Mt. Hood, (now titled Journey to the Soul) put on by Gary Zukav and Linda Francis. I had read Gary's *Seat of the Soul* book in the mid-1990's, long before the plane crash, but never took the opportunity to explore it further until now. It was like a beacon of light calling our names.

To use the program's vernacular, I wanted to align my soul with my personality and I wanted an avenue to continue on my spiritual journey. I wanted what I viewed Linda and Gary as having, and intuitively felt this would be another fork in the road. In the end, I realized that they could never validate me; only I could validate myself. But it was a safe stepping-stone for me at that time.

It was at this program that we were introduced to the idea of a spiritual partnership. What's the difference between a marriage and a spiritual partnership? In the eyes of the law, at least in Canada, probably nothing, but in the eyes of God and in our eyes, it was the firm foundation from which we both wanted to continue our spiritual journey together.

Given the divorce rates and seemingly unhappy relationships that dissolve faster than they were created in the first place, I knew that I didn't want to be involved in or be married into a relationship that didn't serve my spiritual journey. It's the intention behind the partnership that holds the lure for me. I knew that I couldn't go back to the traditional sort of marriage with the illusion that it would be equal; I knew as well that all my old limiting beliefs around being subservient to men while no longer held true for me, and would not serve me along my path to freedom.

I also knew that the financial differences between Robin and myself could potentially keep me locked in fear that he was after my money, which is based on fear that I am not capable of being loved for exactly who I am. It also meant I had to learn to share my wealth without making it a form of power and control; like I felt Terry did with me. The program very nicely pointed out for me all the areas in which I had limited myself by believing certain things that, from a spiritual perspective, I had to let go of to grow and be in alignment with my soul's purpose.

The Spiritual Partnership Guidelines are as follows (they are also listed on Gary's website, www.seatofthesoul.com). I've outlined them below for you to understand the basis for what would be my relationship with Robin.

o   **Commitment**: Making my spiritual growth my highest priority.
o   **Courage**: Stretching myself beyond the limited perspectives of the frightened parts of my personality.
o   **Compassion**: Seeing others and myself as souls who sometimes have frightened parts of their personality active.
o   **Conscious Communications and Actions**: Striving to make all my interactions conscious and loving.

My multisensory perception, or some call it intuition, was screaming at me in a nice way that this was true and that if I could just get out of my head and stay closer to my heart, I will see how unconditional love can flourish. I was learning to align my soul's desires, which were harmony, peace cooperation, sharing and a reverence for life with my personality traits, which included both the love side and the fearful side. Under love, I have joy, peace, creativity, abundance, peace, and harmony. Under fear, I have inferiority/superiority, jealousy, anger, resentment, and judgments, to name a few.

I was just now more aware than ever that in order for me to come from my authentic self -the choice of coming from love or coming from fear is always my choice to make ... my conscious choice.

I took the ultimate step and formalized my spiritual partnership with Robin on August 11, 2009. Jim and Lois came out from Kingston to be our witnesses. It was truly a beautiful day; in the morning a thunderstorm rolled through, but by two in the afternoon, the clouds had parted and only sunshine illuminated our way. God was smiling down on us!

Chapter Twenty-Nine—The Crack in the Sidewalk: A Full-Circle Forgiving Moment

Once again, my body aches as I peel away yet another layer of the onion. A mere five days after my final operation, in September 2008, I am wracked with fits of crying and outbursts of uncontrollable anger. However, it is still the emotional pain that has me crippled. Something has finally come full circle for me—something that I really needed to heal on this journey of mine.

I had been resisting this wave, this ugly part of my own personality for the longest time. I didn't want to forgive my dad for all the perceived injustices he did to me as a child. Now, I knew I had to love him unconditionally, which meant I had to accept all of his human frailties—particularly insofar as I had repeated, in my own life, some of the things that my dad had done. I just didn't want it to be true in me. Judge not lest ye be judged!

I had to reclaim my power with my dad. It didn't mean I have to accept any poor behavior on his part. It simply meant I could still own my power and say what was true for me. I wasn't going to enable his poor behavior any more. I could let go of the pain, the anger, the hurt, and the disappointments for all that I felt was missing from my childhood.

My parents did their very best with their level of consciousness. I had intellectually known this, but there's a difference in *thinking* you know the answer and actually *feeling* the answer in your heart. I know without a shadow of a doubt that we were meant to learn this together in this lifetime.

From so much pain came my freedom. I mean this sincerely. If we all could only accept our families for who and what they are and love them anyway, we would be much better off. As the saying goes, we can choose our friends, but we can't choose our families. Probably because those of us that want to blame others for our faults would choose to not be around their family!

However— and it's a big lesson—we incarnate together for exactly those reasons: so we might expand our own version of ourselves. I made this final connection and could now feel clearly how my behavior of not speaking my truth has always enabled my dad's bad behavior. I say bad, because it wasn't getting him what he wanted either, meaning any sort of relationship with me. I had a wall up instead of a healthy boundary.

I could literally feel the pain and anger in my liver (the master gland and the store for anger), and then this too literally melted away.

Just before my foot operation, I went to see my mom in North Vancouver, who at eighty-three was living full-time in a dementia facility. I felt such compassion for her as I very patiently repeated the same answers to her repeated questions. It was very sad to see my once-vibrant mother, who used to take such pride and care in her clothes, hair, and makeup, be caged in her own thoughts, without even really understanding what was happening to her.

I thought back to all the loving things and special times I had with my mom and I felt a deep sadness that this was now her final journey. She would never again be the mother I once knew. I accepted her condition, because I knew from a much larger viewpoint it was her journey alone to take, not mine. All I could do was love her unconditionally in that state.

She had spent the past twenty years of her life alone because she and my dad separated, but never got divorced. Years after this all happened, she would say to me, "I can remember the crack in the sidewalk when I finally put my foot down and said enough is enough. I'm not going to take this abuse anymore." She was emotionally stifled for much of her married life to my dad. So with uncharacteristic power and conviction, after finding some evidence of my father's infidelity; she had the locks changed on the house. Suffice it to say, she finally had the courage to set her own healthy boundaries.

Only flash forward twenty years: she made only one major decision, one that I was now looking at in the mirror and seeing as my potential. She let my dad back in, but held onto her anger, resentment, and bitterness. She was always the fixer and the peacekeeper in the family, and she never wanted to stir things up by telling my dad her truth. If she tried, and I know she did, he wasn't able to receive it and thus provide unconditional love back to support her. Instead, she held all this anger and frustration inside of her.

Louis Hay's book *You Can Heal Your Life* says, "Alzheimer's probable cause is a refusal to deal with the world as it is." Hopelessness, helplessness, and anger set into her body. Her healthy boundaries were still being violated even though she did not live with my dad anymore. Life for our family never changed despite their separation. Both parents still came to every family occasion; the only difference was that the bitterness on both sides grew more evident. No one ever discussed it; it was like nothing happened. Certainly if we tried to talk to my dad about it, he made his steadfast refusal to admit that he was at all at fault. My mother's version was, "Well, you know your father." She never really said words to put him down, but from what she didn't say, I always knew what she meant.

Sadly, I think my dad really did and does love my mom. Because his father died when he was young, he also grew up with conditional love. He never really had the tools, the communication skills, or the awareness to make better decisions, or to be vulnerable and to acknowledge his own shadow self.

Of course, on my spiritual path I understand now that his pain was greater than her pain, but he bullied and tried to control her into believing his own fears and limiting beliefs. She was his enabler as well. Now I could see that I was following in my mom's footsteps if I let it continue.

One night Robin and I were watching the movie *The Notebook*, which is the story of an older man recounting the life he once shared with his wife, the love of his life, after her mind was lost in dementia. This triggered a very real emotion in me that I never saw coming. I cried and cried all night long. Robin simply held me and listened to me as I let out the sadness for my mom's condition and for my part in continuing the charade with my dad. I knew our watching the movie had not been a coincidence; once again, the universe was showing me the truth I needed to see.

The next day, I woke up feeling rather down. Not only did the crying take its toll on me, but also I faced yet another day of just lying around in bed. Robin and I argued about something minor, and before I knew it, I was unleashing more wailing and more fits of anger, all directed at Robin, but not *about* him at all. He may have been the catalyst, but my childhood nightmares came flooding back to me in waves of pain.

My father's eightieth birthday was coming up at the end of October and the family was going to surprise him over the Thanksgiving long weekend. Unfortunately, my father made it known to my brother Rick, who decided to tell me, that I was invited, but Robin wasn't.

I had stewed on that for a few weeks, once again trying to determine why my father would take such a stand. At the very least, it might be a good opportunity for my family to get to know Robin and vice versa. Our spiritual partnership ceremony had taken place a month before, and because we chose to keep it simple and small, our families had not been invited.

"I remember the crack in the sidewalk when I made up my mind" reverberated in my head. I reclaimed my power that day by remembering that it was my choice how I reacted when my dad did what he always did. No matter how many times I would try and tell him my truth, no matter the circumstances, he was always going to be the same. It was me that was going to have to change. I don't mean that I had to accept his bad behaviors, but I could choose to react differently!

Robin had no harsh feelings one way or the other; he only wanted to support me in whatever would make me happy.

All these years, I was confused, thinking if I said what was on my mind and he took exception to it, then I must have done something wrong; I must not be a very good daughter; I must not be very loving, kind, or compassionate. In truth I was all those things, but Dad refused to see it.

I know that I have forgiven him and myself for all the miscommunications we've had; forgiving him is a gift I gave to myself. Forgiveness is giving up the hope that the past could have been any different. I can also see the ugly parts of me in him that I have just realized and accepted in myself. Now more than ever, I have to love him unconditionally, even if he can't love me back unconditionally. This will be an ongoing process for me, but I'll take it one moment at a time. I know I have to keep my heart open, because it's unhealthy for me not to speak up and to say what I need in front of my father. I also know it's more than okay to have my own healthy boundaries. Finally, I realized that I didn't have to pretend anymore. I matter in this world. I am worthy of love ... unconditional love.

Once again, my body responded beautifully when I listened and made this connection. The price I was paying for continuing this charade was being felt in my first three chakras. I could feel my anger subside; more loving thoughts about my dad replaced my old harsh criticisms of him.

A good couple of years later, after a session with my Belief Change Practitioner during which we worked on acknowledging my residue of anger and upset about my dad, I once again had a vivid golf dream. This time, I was alone with my dad engulfed in a very large sand trap, one that I couldn't see out of. My dad kept hitting the plastic ball, but whatever shot he was trying to make he would miss, and he'd cry, "I'm sorry Jill. Oh, I'm so sorry. I'll try again." This happened over and over again and each time, I would go retrieve the ball, bring it back to him and say with great patience and understanding "That's okay, Dad; try again."

He was also completely naked. I saw him as stripped of all his social masks as well. He was asking for forgiveness of me. It was a plastic ball and not a real one, which represented the superficial part of our real life game that we had played all our lives. I was an adult and he was the older version of my dad in this dream.

I awoke refreshed and feeling like I had once and for all forgiven my dad and myself at the heart level.

The crack was narrowing so that all I had to do was easily step to the other side. So I put one foot in front of the other, picked up the pieces of my life, and simply kept walking forward. All of this came about due to my continued meditation practise. In my daily prayers and intentions I say, *"My body moves with ease, comfort, and grace, and I let go of all things that don't serve me any longer, including holding onto anger and past limiting beliefs. I rejoice in all the good I create and let the universe dance within me."* I alone am responsible for the discomfort in my body that I go through every time I feel unworthy and don't speak my truth. It takes a lot of honesty and willingness to look in the mirror and see the truth.

Still, if I'm feeling any discomfort in my body, I have to ask myself what the situation or event needs me to learn. I am supposed to live from my higher or expanded version of myself, so how am I not expanding—or so often in my case, what do I need to be right about? If I can let go, let God, and be in the vortex, be on the side of love instead of fear, then the universe will conspire to give me exactly what I desire and seek!

Serenity, peace, and happiness are just on the other side for those willing to see the crack as merely a fine line. How deep or wide the crack is will be up to each of us. When we narrow the gap and move toward the center, it's only a fine line between love and fear. However, it is through this fine line that the light shines through and to which I am now drawn.

After four years, I'm finally feeling when I meet new people that I can introduce myself and I know who I am. I don't have to apologize for anything; in fact I am extremely appreciative of all that has happened. It is my story, but it doesn't have to define me or be my cross to bear. Instead, it was an incredible opportunity that has taught me that this was to be my destiny.

Through all pain and suffering comes hope and opportunity. I only pray that by sharing my story you might find a connection to an event in your own life that can take you from a place of being a victim to being a victor, a warrior for your own life.

Change and uncertainty are certainly paralyzing thoughts if we let them be. Having the courage to change our perspectives and our limiting beliefs is not easy, but it is each soul's journey—and it is worth it. It is a process and a journey all at the same time. Life will never be perfect; in fact, there is perfection in imperfection. This connection is what gave me my path to freedom. All paths lead to one place: love. Love yourself, for exactly who you are, and love others just the same.

Namaste: the divine in me acknowledges the divine in you.

Epilogue

The Law of Karma -
"Every action generates a force of energy that
returns to us in like kind ... what we sow is
what we reap. And when we choose actions
that bring happiness and success to others, the
fruit of our karma is happiness and success."
—Deepak Chopra

As the writing of my book neared a close, my Belief Change Practitioner, Beverly Lenz, introduced me to a lady who channels Archangel Michael. Intuitively, Beverly felt I would find some benefit in an angel reading.

I contacted the person by phone and was advised to e-mail her my questions. She preferred not to meet me in person. She explained that she would go into a meditative state in which she could channel the angel. It only occurred to me after I had completed writing this book that maybe I should see what the angels had to say about my karmic tie with Robin. Maybe there was something more to our journey, so I asked

"What is my karmic tie with my present husband, Robin? What lessons are we to learn together?"

She sent the angel's reply. I copy it here in its entirely.

You and Robin have had many lifetimes together,
each one working on a different aspect of yourselves
for your spiritual evolution. Most of your lessons have

been learned. However, there is one remaining bit of karma that has not been completed, and this is the main focus for your time together in this incarnation. In the early 1800's, there was a lifetime in Paris, France, in which you were the best of friends. You were both male and quite taken with yourselves. You drank together, gambled together, fought together, and chased women together. Both of you lived in spoiled luxury with your puffed-up egos until one day, a woman caught your attention. Both of you pursued her with wild abandonment, yet she refused both of your advances. The fact that both of you wanted her, yet she would have nothing to do with either one of you, caused you to blame each other, which eventually caused so much anger between you that it ruined your lifelong friendship and you never spoke to each other again. Each of you truly missed the other, yet your foolish pride never allowed you to end the quarrel and let bygones be bygones. You missed the lesson of unconditional love and forgiveness completely, and you both died bitter and alone. Had you cherished each other more than the attention of an unattainable woman, you would have had a lifetime of true friendship and companionship with each other that would have made your lives rich and full and happy instead of sad, lonely, and bitter.

You have a chance now to find that unconditional love and forgiveness that you denied yourselves then. When you find you have feelings of competition or jealousy or even resentment that come out of nowhere in this lifetime, stop and get quiet together and say this simple phrase: "I forgive you for everything you have done to me in the past, present, and future, and I forgive myself for everything I have done to you in the past, present, and future, and we are surrounded by the unconditional love of God." It is simply miraculous what these few words can do for you. Immediately, you have changed the past where the problem began, you have changed your present circumstances, and you have changed forever the future relationships you will ever encounter with each other.

Is it a coincidence that neither Robin nor I drinks or gambles, or that we are completely faithful to each other? Each of us only wants peace and harmony in our relationship, after our long-ago puffed-up egos brought us both to our knees and made us humble enough to respect the other's own unique spiritual path. Just like the reading I had done when I was twenty-one, it confirms for me that through karma we are all tied to one another, and we as souls have come here to learn certain lessons.

Resources

The following is a list of the top twenty-five books that inspired me the most during my recovery process (not in preferential order).

1. Walsch, Neal Donald. *Conversations with God: An Uncommon Dialogue*
2. Walsch, Neal Donald. *Happier than God*
3. Walsch, Neal Donald. *When Everything Changes Change Everything*
4. Chopra, Deepak. *How to Know God*
5. Chopra, Deepak. *The Spontaneous Fulfillment of Desire: Harnessing the Infinite Power of Coincidence*
6. Chopra, Deepak. *The Seven Spiritual Laws of Success*
7. Chopra, Deepak. *The Path to Love: Renewing the Power of Spirit in your Life*
8. Taylor, Jill Bolte. *My Stroke of Insight: A Brain Scientist's Personal Journey*
9. Millman, Dan. *Way of the Peaceful Warrior*
10. Hicks, Esther and Jerry. *The Vortex: Where the Law of Attraction Assembles All Cooperative Relationships*
11. Montgomery, Darlene. *Dream Yourself Awake*
12. Ford, Debbie. *The Dark Side of the Light Chasers*
13. Lad, Dr. Vasant, *Ayurveda: The Science of Self-Healing*
14. Toile, Eckhart. *The Power of Now: A Guide to Spiritual Enlightenment*
15. Toile, Eckhart. *A New Earth: Awakening to Your Life's Purpose*
16. *Zukav, Gary. The Seat of the Soul*

17. *Zukav, Gary and Linda Francis. The Heart of the Soul: Emotional Awareness*

18. *Zukav, Gary and Linda Francis. Spiritual Partnerships*

19. Levine, Barbara Hoberman. *Your Body Believes Every Word You Say: The Language of the Body/Mind Connection*

20. Rushnell, Squire. *When God Winks: How the Power of Coincidence Guides Your Life*

21. Dooley, Mike. *Infinite Possibilities: The Art of Living Your Dreams*

22. Dooley, Mike. *Choose Them Wisely: Thoughts Become Things!*

23. Lipton, Bruce H. and Steve Bhaerman. *Spontaneous Evolution: Our Positive Future*

24. Singer, Michael A. *The Untethered Soul: The Journey Beyond Yourself*

25. Hay, Louise I. *You Can Heal Your Life*

About the Author

Writing about my true story of surviving a plane crash and starting over at the age of forty-seven has been a cathartic journey. The lengthy recovery process was the best thing that ever happened to me; allowing me time to reflect on the important things in my life and what was really missing. My search for that elusive purpose in life was finally answered as I dug through many layers of traumas and dramas that made up my life up until that point. It had nothing to do with all my accomplishments, jobs, titles, or material stuff that I had spent my entire life striving for and achieving.

Learning to trust, forgive and to love unconditionally both others and myself has been the biggest step toward freedom and personal peace I have ever taken. I know I was given a second chance on life and it was up to me what I was going to do with this incredible opportunity to literally re-write my life and thus my story.

My greatest source of joy – *knowing* that I am not alone and that I am connected to my source, the one power I call God.

My full recovery allows me to once again enjoy an active life. Golf challenges me still, but in a different way. I love yoga, meditating, reading, biking, hiking, hospice work and just being!

I love continuing to expand who I am. I spend more time simply honoring myself, my body and the "me" in some might say the old silly Jilly, but I prefer the new joyful Jilly.

My spiritual partnership with Robin, the owner of those eyes that were illuminated in my husband's eyes minutes before we crashed is the most challenging and loving relationship I have ever had, because it requires so much honesty with the real me—no masks allowed.

Mostly, I've learned to surrender to the dance of the Universe and to just let God show me the way. What a relief.

joyfuljilly@gmail.com

CPSIA information can be obtained at www.ICGtesting.com
Printed in the USA
LVOW080801110512

281247LV00001B/15/P